SEASONS
OF THE
EARTH
AND
HEART

Becoming Aware of Nature, Self, and Spirit

WILLIAM J. FITZGERALD
Foreword by Joyce Rupp, O.S.M.

AVE MARIA PRESS
NOTRE DAME, INDIANA 46556

© 1991 by Ave Maria Press, Notre Dame, IN 46556

International Standard Book Number: 0-87793-456-8 (pbk.)
0-87793-457-6

Library of Congress Catalog Card Number: 91-72453

Cover and text design by Katherine Robinson Coleman

Printed and bound in the United States of America.

DEDICATION

This book is dedicated
to Kateri and to Black Elk
whose blessings for this book
I sought from the four directions
at the Tower of the Four Winds,
and to John Paul I, the smiling Pope,
whose blessing I received in Rome.

ACKNOWLEDGMENTS

. . . to my friends at the Franciscan Renewal
Center, Scottsdale, Arizona

. . . to my friend Sister Susan Severin, RSM, and
her library staff at the College of St. Mary,
Omaha, Nebraska

. . . and to Jim Ely my friend and Frank
Cunningham my editor for their invaluable
assistance

CONTENTS

FOREWORD

Many strong, vivid memories came rushing into my consciousness as I read *Seasons of the Earth and Heart*. I felt drawn to the earth, back to my years of growing up on a farm in rural Iowa. There I had experienced the four seasons over and over with their great bursts of heat and their barbs of bitter cold. There I saw seeds planted in field after field. There I witnessed summer storms wipe out an entire crop one year and the summer sun bring a golden harvest the next. I was one with the earth in so many ways in those youthful times. I never separated myself from the seasons. They were a part of me and I of them.

I had a father who loved the land, who treated it gently and who walked upon it with pride. I remember so well a time when I was walking with him by one of the fields in the dew of early morning. He paused by the edge of the newly plowed field with its dark soil. He stooped down, picked up a handful of the black earth and held it close to his face. As he smelled its rich, musty odor his face held a beautiful expression of satisfaction. He never spoke a word but I learned so much in that moment of communion with the land that he loved.

I also remember a time of spring plowing when my father accidentally uncovered a nest of baby rabbits in the furrows. He put the motherless creatures in his tool box and brought them home to us. We gladly nourished them with our baby doll bottles full of milk and eventually gave the rabbits back to the fields. It was a way of learning to reverence all creatures.

The same was true of our farm home where both strangers and friends were always invited to come and share a meal with us. We knew the power of laughter and the joy of friendship as some of the greatest treasures of life.

A very contrasting memory also returned to me as I read this book. It was of a more recent time when I was sitting by the front door of a home in the slums of the capital city of Liberia. I had drawn my chair to the door that morning, knowing that I needed to pray about the depression and desolation I felt in seeing the poverty and disease of the city.

I sat there for a long, long time while I pondered the piles of trash I saw and smelled. I watched the crowd walking down the bumpy, rain-pocked street full of deep holes. I sat looking at the groups of thin people with their little shacks for markets, trying to make enough for one more day of life. I hurt for them and for the earth upon which they walked. I could not find beauty there. I struggled with the brokenness of that place. The disharmony I felt within myself was distressing.

My stay in the slums of Liberia was such a contrast from my youth. Yet, both of these life situations connected me with humanity. It is this truth that William Fitzgerald writes about in *Seasons of the Earth and Heart*. He looks at the dualisms of life, those opposites that seem to have no commonality, and sees the possibility for hope and growth there. His creative approach to the four seasons makes this possibility believable.

I was drawn into the stories of the people William Fitzgerald writes about. It is especially through the powerful descriptions of ordinary people he has known that one senses the beauty of the earth and the power of a single person to transform it. These people of wisdom and integrity contribute harmony to a world of great discordance. They have seen and touched the sacred in the most common of things and experiences. They have made deliberate choices on how to relate to life. Because of this they have known the circle of oneness and the power of the arrow of love.

The richness of our Native American spiritual heritage with its tremendous reverence for all of life permeates this book. It helps one to make sense out of the opposites that fill our days. Life will continue to be composed of both joys and sorrows, of good and evil, of life and death. Fitzgerald's is a book about mending the opposites of life, of discovering a oneness and a union that is possible as we travel through the seasons. It is both comforting and challenging. It is a book to be pondered and taken to heart.

It is our time now to contribute to the transformation of the world. There are more and more people who are attentive to the inner journey and to the care of the earth. These two go hand in hand. As we are transformed and brought into the circle of harmony so will we have the desire for the arrow of love to move us from a people of conflict and war to a people of compassion and unity. We will always have some evil pressing against our goodness but the more reverence we have for life the less effect evil can have upon us.

We can accept the tremendous contribution of our Native Americans' spirituality and walk with greater reverence upon the earth and with the peoples of the earth. Whether we live in a densely populated city or in a sparsely populated countryside we must seek to find our inner harmony and to share that harmony with the universe. *Seasons of the Earth and Heart* invites us to this journey.

—Joyce Rupp, O.S.M.

INTRODUCTION

Spirituality is a way to the powers of the universe: if you settle for less, you end up in the
profound pathology of risking the planet.

—Brian Swimme, Physicist

Seasons of the Earth and Heart is about earthy spirituality.
It is about the powers of the earth—water, wind, and
fire—speaking to us. It is about the seasons of the earth
and the seasons of our heart nudging into our consciousness. Within it are stories, poems, reflections, and prayer
experiences about the allurement and pursuit of genuine
beauty in our lives.

It suggests that we look at creation anew, if only in
our imaginations. After all, most of us are boxed in concrete, glass, and steel cities, with only our imaginations
to take us into the fullness of creation.

It suggests we discover again the spiritually energetic and creative people who have their feet on the
earth and their eyes toward the sun. Some are visionaries, some are our neighbors. They share spiritualities
that love creation.

It suggests we recognize that there are ancient
prayer tracks over America that deserve our respect.
These were left by the first Americans and have been
too long excluded from our awareness and reverence.
While we cannot presume to enter into the fullness of
their own experience, we can learn some deep lessons
of reverence from their journeys and their lives. Their
earthy stories make no extravagant claims; they represent people who have known both sin and brokenness, but who, in the midst of their suffering, reverenced
creation.

It suggests that we discover again the spiritual energy of holy places—the holy mountains and holy water where people search for wholeness. If the journey of spirituality is, according to Swimme, "to discover the allurement in the universe and the allurement in us," we must start looking in the places of cosmic energy and beauty, and in the dwellings of energetic, creative, and loving persons. When we discover these, we will be on holy ground.

Seasons of the Earth and Heart is about the circle—a metaphor for life and nature. Life is a sacred circle. Our first stories were probably told as the first humans sat in a circle around a campfire. The seasons are a circle. Life itself circles from birth to growth to death. Through the eons the circle has appeared everywhere: at Stonehenge, on the Peruvian heights, and on the plains of North America.

We all bring brokenness to the circle. Wherever a human circle gathers, and the truth is told, we discover we are all broken in some way: broken hearts, dreams, self-images. Sometimes we are broken by sin. Sometimes our health is broken. We all need spiritual energy and healing. So we gather in healing circles—AA, base communities, RENEW groups. This book is about drawing the circle together.

Seasons of the Earth and Heart is about the arrow—a symbol of the cross, the arrow of love, full of power. With its piercing power it entered the circle of life and mother earth trembled and the skies wept. The Celts symbolized this with their cross—a cross ringed with a circle that is rooted in the ancient world of the druids who reverenced the circle of life.

Without the circle of earth there could be no cross. Without the cross there could be no fulfillment of the circle. We will appreciate the glory of the cross better if we reverence the encircling arms of mother earth who held the cross.

Seasons of the Earth and Heart is a search for the arrow of the cross in the center of the holy earth. Start reading anywhere you like. Perhaps in the current season of the year or in the season of your heart at this moment. Each chapter is followed by reflection questions and a theme prayer. Poems are interspersed throughout.

You can use the book for a personal journey by using the suggested images at the end of each segment for personal prayer. If you care to keep a journal, there are statements at the end of each segment with which to start your journal entries (you will need a separate notebook).

Each segment opens with a scripture quote, followed by a true story drawn from the sparkling sea of stories that make up our lives. Connect the scripture and these stories with your own, and enjoy the creation of a new connection in the great circle.

All is beautiful,
All is beautiful,
All is beautiful, indeed.
Now the Mother Earth
And the Father Sky,
Meeting, joining one another,
Helpmates ever they.
All is beautiful,
All is beautiful,
All is beautiful, indeed.

Navaho Poem

1

THE ARROW
IN THE CIRCLE

He made me into a sharpened arrow, and concealed me in his quiver.

— Isaiah 49:2

At the beginning, we know there was light. The fireball hurled out light that still races through the cosmos. Such a holy moment, such a holy light! "The light shines in the darkness, and the darkness has not overcome it," writes John in his gospel.

Every element in the universe was in some way present in the eruption of the fireball. From the beginning there was a kinship of all matter. Planet earth, a tiny speck among the hurling orbits, rushed into life. She was a special blessing, thrusting up mountains and pushing forth glaciers and sprinkling rain—holy water. Insofar as we know, earth is the only wellspring of liquid water in the universe!

Some 3.5 billion years ago bacterial life stirred in the earth's womb of water. Millions of years later plants appeared in the sea. Millions of years beyond that, plants came ashore and eventually flowers appeared. They spread a path of beauty that would one day welcome humans. Planet earth bloomed and all was holy.

All of this occurred millions of years before sin. Sin was the legacy of the upright humans. They broke relationships and abused blessings. But even after sin the humans walked upon the holy earth leaving their footprints pressed upon the soil for they were "down to earth folk," kinfolk to their mother and to all the other creatures.

In their hearts there was a yearning for the sacred circle. From the beginning, there was wholeness in the circle. There was a healing there. The mid-point of the circle was the center of the universe for the early peoples. The medicine wheel of the Native Americans, a circle of healing rocks, has a history that spirals back into the mists of antiquity.

There was also a caution in the circle. About 300 B.C., the author of the book of Ecclesiastes would lament the fatalism derived from the circle as the only image of the human spiritual journey:

> What does man gain by all the toil at which he toils under the sun? A generation goes, and a generation comes, but the earth remains forever. The sun rises and the sun goes down and hastens to the place where it rises. The wind blows to the south, and goes around to the north; round and round goes the wind, and on its circuits the wind returns.... All things are full of weariness.... What has been is what will be, and what has been done is what will be done; and there is nothing new under the sun (Eccl 1:3–6, 8–9).

After eons of evolution, after human consciousness had developed a longing for something or someone new, in the fullness of time, there was someone new in the circle. That which is beyond and more than we could ever dream, entered in a new way, personally at the center of the circle.

And the Word became flesh and dwelt among us, full of grace and truth; we have beheld his glory... (Jn 1:14).

The incarnation meant a revolution within evolution. The birth, life, death, and resurrection of Jesus Christ were a leap into what love and life might become. This meant a breakthrough of hope, of salvation; a breaking into human consciousness and human history of the reign of God.

The arrow symbolizes this breakthrough. The cross of Jesus is a new arrow in the circle of creation, an arrow that pierces to the heart of matter. The arrow image carries strength, power, directness, convergence, and a wounding. So does the cross.

The arrow of Christ's cross is a sign of contradiction. It pierced the earth and brought death, but it bore love and opened up life. It was a saving arrow in the center of all history, a revolutionary beauty burst upon the timeless evolutionary scene—something radically new and glorious.

The cross is an arrow of love that trembled the earth with its piercing. The winds of Good Friday swept into Easter, rolling back the stone and hurling light into the darkest corners of death.

The passion, death, and resurrection of Jesus Christ were something new in the circle. The universe could never be the same again after these cosmic events.

In the unfolding of time, our understanding of this power and beauty of the circle of creation and the arrow of salvation widens. Earth and cross are joined at the point of suffering. From this point they radiate sympathy and compassion.

Christians, however, have too often ignored the connection between circle and cross. We have held the cross aloft, aloof from earth, disdaining the earth circle below. Witness the 500 years of Christian European conquest of the new world and its native peoples who were so close to the earth.

However, a special cross does keep the arrow of the cross at mid-point in the circle. Its very imagery illustrates closeness between cross and circle and can be a wonderful symbol of what Jurgen Moltmann refers to when he writes that "... the Kingdom of God is also the kingdom of universal sympathy for all things."

It is the Celtic cross, a cross ringed by a circle. It bridges the old world of the circle and the new world of the gospel. It has its roots in the old world of Christian Europe and in the ancient world of the Celtic druids who reverenced the circle of life. At a time when we violate the circle, when the ozone burns away at the poles and the rain forests disappear at the center, the Celtic cross reminds us of a spirituality of creation.

The exact symbolism of the Celtic cross is lost in antiquity. The circle may stand for the sun, or the earth; circling the cross of Christ it symbolizes tremendous energy proclaiming glory and beauty. In the shadow of the Celtic cross, the Celts could pray:

> Every seed will take root in the earth...
> I will come round with my step,
> I will go rightways with the sun.

Perhaps the Celtic cross is the best image of the arrow in the circle. Is it far-fetched to relate this cross to the Native Americans and their spirituality? In his excellent book *Voices of Earth and Sky*, Vinson Brown writes:

...I believe the Celts and particularly the Irish Celts were closest in spirit to the Native Americans. They were an earth and sky people in the old days....

This book is also about earth and sky people and the beauties of North America. When we get back to earth and air, water and fire, we approach the center of reality, the essence of life. Brian Swimme, a scientist and mystic points out:

The work of the human is uncovering the superficial allurements. This is the journey of spirituality. It is to discover the allurement in the universe and the allurement in us. It is a dangerous journey, but filled with joy. If you settle for less, you end up with following a path that risks the whole planet.

The arrow of the cross pierces what is superficial. The Celtic cross is a wholistic image that calls us to reverence the beauty of the arrow and the circle.

REFLECTION QUESTIONS:

1) "The incarnation meant a revolution within evolution." What is revolutionary about the message of Jesus in our times?

2) There is "allurement in the universe." Gravity, the tides, the flowers reaching toward the sun all reveal a deep allurement built into the universe. What are some of the deep allurements built into human existence?

3) The journey of spirituality uncovers superficial allurements. How do we distinguish the superficial from the real? How does the cross of Jesus direct us to the heart of reality? What are the allurements in your own life that give promise of lasting joy?

CROSSROADS PRAYER

O Lord, may I walk with beauty. May I meet you at the
crossroads of
>   integrity and truth,
>   compassion and justice,
>   craftsmanship and quality,
>   suffering and fortitude,
>   where faith and hope are intersected by love.

O Lord, may I discover you at the center-point.
Deliver me from idolizing the superficial and from the
>   glamor of evil,
>   tyranny of appearance,
>   fallacy of hype,
>   greed of advertising,
>   and the manipulation of propaganda.

And when the good road crosses the path of difficulties,
>   be the arrow that points the way.
>   May I walk with beauty before me;
>   may I walk with beauty behind me;
>   may I walk with beauty all around me!

Beauty at the Center
Black Elk

Ask, and it will be given you; seek, and you will
find; knock, and it will be opened to you.

— Matthew 7:7

In 1863—the winter when the four crows were killed—a
great holy man of the Ogalala Sioux was born near the
Powder River in Montana. His name was Black Elk.

At age nine, while encamped near the Little Bighorn
River, Black Elk was seized by a serious illness, during which he had a mysterious and powerful vision.
Throughout the rest of his long life, he would "seek"
and try to "find" the ultimate meaning of the vision. In
his last years he would share his vision with the poet
laureate of Nebraska, John Neihardt, who recorded it in
his book *Black Elk Speaks*.

Black Elk tells of being caught up in a dream and
taken into the skies by two men riding out of the clouds.
Appearing with spears of jagged lightning they tell him
that the grandfathers are calling him. From the four
compass points the sky is filled with dancing horses.
A beautiful rainbow points to a teepee containing six
grandfathers and they invite him to a great vision. As
he rides out to his greater vision, the sky is filled with
prancing horses of bay, red, black, and yellow. He
glimpses his people below on earth, walking under a
healthy tree, but later there is calamity and his people are
scattered.

Still, hope remained in the vision; he saw the day-
star arise in the east and a mighty bison appeared. He

was given a mission, to plant a new tree of understanding filled with beautiful birds. Below him, the sacred hoop of the Sioux, which had been shattered, was whole again, and there were present the hoops of other peoples, and encircling all, one great hoop of understanding:

> Then I was standing on the highest mountain of them all and round about beneath me was the whole hoop of the world. And while I stood there, I saw more than I can tell and I understood more than I saw; for I was seeing in a sacred manner the shapes of things in the spirit, and the shape of all shapes as they must live together like one being. And I saw that the sacred hoop of my people was one of many hoops that made one circle, wide as daylight and as starlight, and in the center grew one mighty flowering tree to shelter all the children of one mother and one father. And I saw that it was holy (*Black Elk Speaks*).

In 1890, Black Elk received another powerful vision while dancing the ghost dance at Wounded Knee Creek, South Dakota. An eagle, sacred harbinger to the native peoples, took him through the skies to a sacred tree. There twelve men told him he was to meet a holy person. This glorious man, from whom colored rays of light shone, said that all earth creatures and growing things belong to him.

These visions would stay with Black Elk all his life, but he would also suffer much anguish as to how they would be lived out in the lives of his people. In 1947, Joseph Epes Brown sought out the holy man and found him in an old canvas-walled tent on a Nebraska farm. Brown subsequently spent the winter with him at Black Elk's family home, a hewn-log cabin, near Manderson, South Dakota. The old man had seen eighty-five winters. During that winter, he confided the sacred rites of the

Ogalala Sioux which Brown recorded in his book, *The Sacred Pipe*. Black Elk describes the sacred rite of the sweat lodge and the door to the teepee being opened for the last time:

> . . .it is the wish of Wakan-Tanka that the light enters into the darkness that we may see not only with our two eyes, but with the one eye which is of the heart, and with which we see and know all that is true and good.

The gospel tells us: Ask and you shall receive, seek and you shall find. This asking demands great attentiveness to the reality that God is present and the moment is sacred. Brown describes this spirit of attentiveness as "central to the native peoples." Black Elk called it "crying for a vision." Out of this attentiveness came the vision and the prayer of Black Elk:

> Hear me four quarters of the world—a relative I am! Give me the strength to walk the soft earth, a relative to all that is. Give me the eyes to see and the strength to understand that I may be like you. With your power only can I face the winds (*Black Elk Speaks*).

Today, Black Elk and Neihardt are memorialized at a beautiful shrine on top of a bluff overlooking the Missouri River near Blair, Nebraska. The inscription reads:

> This symbolic tower is erected as a tribute to Ogalala Sioux holy man, Black Elk (1863–1950) and to John G. Neihardt (1881–1973), who captured the great visions of Black Elk in his book, *Black Elk Speaks* . . . . The center of the mosaic mural on the face of the TOWER OF THE FOUR WINDS represents a universal messiah figure standing against the tree of life with outstretched arms in benediction over all people. The tree of

life is centered in a circle of light, ever-widening until it reaches the outer circle, the brilliant blue of the sky. In the outer circle, cottonwood leaves are seen with birds flying in to sing in the tree of life.

The crossarms of the design represent the crossing of the roads—the horizontal black road of difficulties that all must walk, and the vertical good red road of life that leads from the great spirit to mother earth. Black Elk said, "The good road and the road of difficulties you have made to cross, and where they cross—that place is holy."

That cross with its beautiful blue, red, and brown mosaics is planted in the very heart of North America. It is a cross within a circle. It is an "arrow in the circle."

Only a very special person could inspire such a memorial. Vinson Brown describes the special qualities of Black Elk this way: "This wonderful human being, pure of heart and a great teacher, managed to keep alive in his heart and mind the beautiful essence of his people and their meaning in the sacred circle of earth and sky."

IMAGINE: Where and when are you most surrounded by beauty? In your family circle? At a place in nature? Be attentive to the beauty there and praise God for such beauty.

JOURNAL: "Asking demands great attentiveness to the reality that God is present and the moment is sacred." I need to be more attentive to . . .

Beauty at the Center
Ultimate Wholeness

Anything happens if we are open to see that creation is coming alive. The real is the beautiful transformed by love and the wonder of new life; turn on right now.

— "Anything Happens"
Monks of Weston Priory

A certain joy emanates from a circle of wholesome people, people who know their own foibles but who are on a quest for authenticity. No wonder King Arthur gathered his jousting knights in such a circle at Camelot. Carl Jung notes that "the symbol of the circle...always points to the single most vital aspect of life, its ultimate wholeness." The very image of the round table refers to a quest for wholeness.

There is joy and laughter around such a round table. It was so at Camelot. It was so at the wedding feast of Cana. A verse often attributed to the English writer Hillaire Belloc says, "Wherever a Catholic sun doth shine, there's always laughter and good red wine, at least I've always found it so, *benedicamus Domino!*"

To see ourselves not as gods, but as a jousting, questing crew around the table is the beginning of a smile. The Sioux have special dancers, a group of fools called Heyokoas, who bring lightness and laughter to their sacred dances by doing everything backwards. They sing a song to the paradoxical human situation. Laughter is a part of their spirituality.

23

An Invitation

Roman Catholics too have sacred ceremonies. Some of the most solemn take place in Saint Peter's basilica in Rome. In ancient times, the crowds around the pope at solemn ceremonies became so large that his attendants started to carry him into Saint Peter's on a portable throne. And at his installation, the pope was crowned by a huge triple-tiered crown.

Pope John Paul I dispensed with the great crown and portable throne and walked into Saint Peter's. He got down to earth. The people saw him up close and they still remember him as "the smiling pope." His smile was an invitation to join the circle; it was a reflection of his gentle humor. While bishop of Venice he wrote light-hearted essays that were dialogs with such fictional characters as Pinnochio and Figaro, even with Mark Twain and the poor. He saw no contradiction between having Christ as the center of his life, while laughter and mirth radiated from that center. His smile was an invitation to join him around that center. He was pope for only a month before his sudden death in September of 1979. Today, his tomb is strewn with flowers daily. The people remember.

The cross is planted in earth. When we get down to earth and put aside our crowns of appearances we can laugh at ourselves. We can smile like John Paul I knowing that we are members of a motley crew, and that the healing of the glorious cross can save even us in our foolishness.

Widening the Circle

When we do get down to earth, we get closer to the poor who are down and "out." John Paul I wrote that we must give preference to them and recognize that rich and poor and everyone in between are part of the human motley crew:

> We are in the same boat, filled with people now brought closer together, both in space and in behavior, but the boat is on a very rough sea. . . . The rule must be this, insist on what unites us and forget what divides us.
>
> — *Illustrissimi*, John Paul I

To widen the circle was the aim of John Paul I. It was precisely the efforts of Jesus to widen the circle to include outsiders that brought down the wrath of the Pharisees. At Cana, Jesus worked his first miracle for a bride and groom who ran out of wine. That young couple would likely have joyfully danced a Hebrew circle wedding dance. Is it far-fetched to imagine a smiling Jesus dancing in that wedding dance, taking part in the energy of that full circle?

Jesus also went out and saw a tax collector, named Levi, sitting at the tax office, and he said to him, "Follow me!" Beyond the celebrating circles of life there is also the sometimes messy world of work. Jesus was in the center of both.

For years, Cesar Chavez tried to raise awareness of the dangers of chemicals used to enhance our food. When asked who was being affected, he responded:

> We are—farm workers, people in rural towns, and consumers. We've got to do something fast before they kill us all!

At that time Chavez undertook a fast. Day after day, he weakened and became emaciated. In looking bad he was doing good.

Today, as we leave the supermarket, the produce still glistens and shines. Recently we learned that some growers applied a toxic chemical to apples to make them bright and shiny. In that same market our eyes are caught at the check-out counter by colorful tabloids proclaiming: "Space Aliens Kidnap Housewife!" The brightly packaged cigarettes make one final appeal. It all looks great. So do we, in our designer jeans. We are all walking billboards advertising something exclusive. We might wonder sometimes who owns whom. Does the buyer own the product, or the product own the buyer?

At that same moment in school, our children may glimpse in a modern history lesson the face of Cesar Chavez or Mother Teresa. Will they know the difference between the truly beautiful and the imitation? Do we?

Closer to home, will the wrinkled faces of grandparents be seen as beautiful? The old are usually portrayed in our media as pathetic or bumbling. Care-lined faces and callused hands are the "real thing." They've been worn down by loving and no advertiser need package them.

On Good Friday Jesus cried out: "I thirst!" Instead of the real thing, they gave him gall.

Once upon a time, there was an unappealing outsider named Zacchaeus whom Jesus invited in.

Once upon a time, there was a pope whose body was entirely too small, but whose smile was worldwide!

Chavez would end his fasts at the eucharist. There, we too can discover the real thing, the bread that nourishes and gives everlasting life.

IMAGINE: Jesus pausing on his journey to taste grapes in his native Galilee; imagine him smiling and smacking his lips. Imagine him stopping at a grape arbor to comfort a tired laborer.

JOURNAL: List the main objects, persons, possessions, growing things, creatures in your home, garage, and yard. When you have listed the many that seem important, go back and underline the six that are of the greatest beauty and lasting value to you, thus separating the genuine and really valuable from the superficial.

Beauty at the Center
An Expanding Circle

Then to all he said, "If anyone wants to be a
follower of mine, let him renounce himself and
take up his cross every day and follow me."

— Luke 9:23 (JB)

HOLY CROSS

Oak Creek's red rocks leap up
and dance a circle in the sun.
    A cross impaled in mountain stone
    throws out its arms in blessing.
A red crowned finch alights on the font,
and laps up the waters of life.
    Swept up in graceful flight,
    to cross's arm—singing, "Beauty!"
Red finch, red rocks, red sunset,
Christ's blood—from arrow spent?

In Oak Creek Canyon in Arizona, a beautiful chapel
perches on a ledge in the side of a crimson canyon wall.
It is the chapel of the Holy Cross, whose unique cross
is like an arrow plunged in the canyon's side. Emerging
from the red rocks below the chapel it rises to become
the center-point of the chapel's south facade.

For the Christian, the cross is an arrow of love. To
fall in love is to know the wound and the passion of
eros. No wonder that the arrow has been a symbol of
love through the ages. Cupid shoots the arrow and the
heart is pierced with love.

The cross is an arrow from the father's quiver

28

allured into the side of mother earth. The earth did not harden its heart and deny it; only people did.

The arrow of the cross in the center of the earth's circle proclaims a cosmic love affair. It is God's passion for earth. For the Christian, the arrow of the cross is in the center of our circle. Taking hold of the cross demands letting go of superficial allurements.

In one of his movies, Bob Newhart plays the role of president of the United States. As he drives through Washington in his bubble-topped limo, he has an artificial arm that extends up through the roof and waves at the crowds as he converses about other matters below. He is disconnected from the people, the very source of his power.

It is easy to become disjointed and disconnected, to replace the real with the artificial, to sail through life in a bubble-topped limo. This was the trap of the Pharisees.

For most of her life, Rosa Parks was one of those black persons that white folks just didn't see from their bubble tops. Rosa burst the bubble one day in Birmingham, Alabama, when she refused to give up her seat to a white man and move to the back of the bus. For that act of courage, she had to take up the double cross of facing the hostility of whites and the disfavor of some of her own people for stirring things up. Her act of courage was really an act of dying to appearances. Because of that act of dying-love, the whole civil rights movement was energized. The heart of Rosa Parks opened up for the great benefit of all of her people.

The arrow of the cross in our circle of life opens up the heart for compassion, for suffering with all humanity and all creation. Our tendency is to let the ego fill the circle and to push all else to the perimeter. To accept the allurement of the cross is to let go and make room in the circle. What first appears as a collapse from the thrust of the arrow is really an opening up.

The daily opening up to the cross can take on heroic proportions. Oscar Romero was ordained as a status quo bishop in El Salvador but he soon began to sense deeply the intense suffering of his people. He was wounded with love and he began to speak daily of compassion and justice. As long as he had dealt with superficialities and looked good he was no problem. The same kind of principalities and powers that could not stomach Christ, could not tolerate the Oscar Romero who advocated justice. He was shot to death while saying Mass.

In Oklahoma there is a parish that sponsored over six thousand refugees over a twelve-year period. It began out of concern for Southeast Asians fleeing Cambodia, Laos, and Vietnam, but eventually welcomed refugees from Albania, Romania, and Zaire. Blessed Sacrament Parish made a special effort to help single men, older persons, and the handicapped since they were the most difficult to sponsor.

Through a slow and difficult adjustment most of the people worked hard to better themselves and settled throughout the country. Wherever they went, the cross on a church steeple meant what it said: an arrow opening into love.

There is a high school very close to Black Elk's shrine where the horizontal road of difficulty and vertical road of the good life cross. It's a holy place, another arrow in the circle, a sanctuary in the inner city of Omaha. Father Flanagan High School is a "MASH unit" caring for the wounded.

Most of its students have been having trouble in school for some time. Some have been expelled from other schools for misbehavior. Many are from broken homes; the majority live in severe poverty. Many have experienced alcoholism and physical abuse. On a yearly average, about one fourth are judged as delinquent by the courts. Some are teen parents. Others are about to be. No student is refused admission because of past difficulty or past labeling.

Father Flanagan High School, which is run by the well-known Boys Town, is an arrow that works in the heart of the inner city. It's an alternative high school offering high risk young people another chance to choose between life on the streets or life as a productive member of society. Its success testifies to the faith of Father Flanagan who believed that deep in the heart of every child was the allurement of the good.

It is also true that throughout human history projectiles—from arrows to heat-seeking missiles—have delivered death. If the cross is an arrow of love, then some sort of dying is also a part of loving. Wherever we are, and in whatever way we allow, the arrow of the cross opens our hearts to compassion. Loving the wounded will always require some kind of dying, some kind of "yes" to the arrow in our circle.

IMAGINE: A circle containing people you work with or with whom you do business. Join hands with the two who are farthest from beauty, most outside the circle. Speak to the Lord about them.

JOURNAL: I cannot rescue the many wounded around me, but I can affirm their basic dignity by . . .

Beauty at the Center
Talking Circles

It was fitting to make merry and be glad, for this
your brother was dead, and is alive; he was lost,
and is found.

— Luke 15:32

The father's welcoming, outstretched arms formed a circle of love for his returning son, a circle of acceptance
and safety. It offered linkage, not domination. Both the
circle of a father's arms and the circle of our mother's
womb are images of wholeness.

The circle is written in the heavens and in our psy-
ches. We find it in all ages and among all peoples: It is
prominent in the Native American medicine wheels and
in their prehistoric petroglyphs found on the southwest-
ern deserts. In some of these places, on the day of the
solstice a shaft of sunlight pierces the center.

We find it in the rose windows of the medieval
cathedrals, Dante's circular journey, Arthur and his
round table, and Ezekiel's fiery wheel. It's possible—
even likely—that Jesus and his disciples reclined in a
circle for the first eucharist. The circle takes everyone in,
offering them safe space.

Talking Circles

The adults gathered in a circle. The leader sat
among them holding a flint arrowhead in his hand. "As I
pass this arrowhead to each of you, reverently receive it
and then speak whatever comes to your mind, whatever
you need to speak now. No judgments will be made. You

32

are safe to speak within the circle. Speak whatever your heart needs to say at this moment."

People spoke and others listened, drawn together by the power of the circle and by holding the arrowhead in common. Somehow, it gave them permission to speak. This was a "talking circle," in the tradition of the Native Americans. Led by a Native American, the participants were a mixed group in a large metropolitan hospital in the southwest, taking part in a holistic health seminar for adults.

That same evening, a few miles away at a Franciscan renewal center, small groups of laypeople also gathered in circles as they had many times before, probing for the meaning of the spiritual life in a world seemingly separated from the spiritual. Warmed by the familiarity and safety of the circle they moved beyond the more traditional understandings of prayer and contemplation to begin to explore a wider circle—the meaning of spirituality in their work lives and in the intimacy of their relationships. That evening they broke new ground and talked about "grounding their spirituality" and how they could put their work and sexuality back in the circle.

Two similar groups used the same approach from different traditions to achieve different goals.

That night, Ron told his story of growth, healing, and spirituality. It is a journey through many talking circles mirroring the mobility of North Americans. It moves west to Japan, east to New York, south to Florida and West Virginia, and west to Arizona. It is a restless story, a turning story, a moving story—a story of the pursuit of beauty.

I probably received my first invitation to pursue beauty while working as an Air Force engineer in Japan. Some Japanese photographers helped me to fall in love with life through a lens. I even came back to art school in New York to get into pictures. I soon realized photography would not offer me the certain financial security and prestige that was more important to me than meaningful work. I turned away from photography and also began to drink heavily.

I was both an engineer and a photographer, but I was restless. I entered med school where I found myself in a group that I enjoyed. Faculty and student dinners provided some camaraderie that was a refuge from the restlessness and boredom that I had felt.

After med school, I had the prestige that went with the title doctor. I moved to West Virginia and picked up another title: assistant professor. Still I was restless and unhappy. My discontent again led me to alcohol then to drugs, seeking the brief peace they could give.

I had no spiritual life. I was financially secure but emotionally and spiritually bankrupt. Soon my physical health was affected. It began to dawn on me that I was a doctor dedicated to saving lives, but in a life-threatening situation myself. My life was out of control. In my mid-thirties, in the prime of life, I was caught up in a cycle of drugs, alcohol, and womanizing. I was like a pinball in a pinball machine, bouncing around and ready to roll off the surface and down the tube.

I felt terrorized, on the brink of losing my values, my career, and myself. In the end the allurements I pursued had no power. The center wasn't holding. The downhill spiral had gone on for thirteen years. Time was flying by and I felt compelled to seek some kind of a spiritual answer. I knew the broken pieces and I thought if I could just put them together, I could go back to God and be accepted. It was still a false view of reality, me pulling myself up by my own bootstraps.

At age thirty-nine, I discovered one of the greatest healing circles in the world. It was a turning point, a spiritual conversion. In that circle, I could say, "Hi! I'm Ron, a recovering alcoholic and addict." Alcoholics Anonymous' twelve steps demanded a reliance on God and this deepened a spiritual hunger in me. I started to search for things of the spirit with a desire to do his will, not just mine. But I was still into lots of head stuff, and property and prestige still got in the way. My will and my self-centeredness still held sway.

I got into a bible study group. It was another good circle, but I still had a tendency to try to manipulate God in order to overcome my wants and needs. I created my own god who could serve my interests. Now that alcohol was dethroned, the Bible became god, rather than a window through which I could glimpse the real God and my real self. I also became harsh in my judgments of those outside this bible circle.

I was led from there into a charismatic prayer group where there was lots of healing and lots of praise, but my life was still compartmentalized. God was to move more into my life. During prayer for those who had a difficulty in developing a relationship with God, I received a baptism of the Holy Spirit. I did experience a powerful presence of the Holy Spirit within. But even after this I still was trying to control God through prayer and healing.

I later attended a Full Gospel men's retreat and the evangelist identified my gifts as a nuclear scientist and that was true because my medical journey and probably my love for photography had led me into radiology. In that circle, I was encouraged to start a family. I was forty-two and had avoided a family because I thought I would be an emotional failure as a husband and a father. I subsequently married and we adopted two boys. I was also assured that God would lead me and show me a direction for a new turn in my life's work.

Throughout this ongoing spiritual journey, the stories of other recovering people told around the circle helped me to keep going. In this journey, I would discover the question at the center of the circle: "What is God's will for me?"

At the mid-point of life I think I really discovered that God's will for me is gracious! I had been a child who was abandoned by his father. The higher power of AA became the father and loving master of my life. I recognized at last that not only the people in the talking circles, but also the father, understood my painful story and accepted me.

Now I enrolled in a bible college at a small charismatic church and attended classes for three years. I was finally beginning to get a firsthand experience of God at work in my life. Out of that, I could let Jesus lead me more and more to the father.

At a retreat in the lake country of Minnesota I came to grips with a deep father wound. I had been carrying this ever since my father had abandoned me as a child. I accepted it as a part of my journey. I now felt the pieces coming together. Like the prodigal son, I could love the heavenly father. Still, in my work, money and security kept pulling me to the peripheral things.

Somehow, throughout this entire journey, my early allurement to photography and the beauty of life still tugged at my heart. This all came together when an opportunity arose to leave hospital practice and open a women's radiology center for the early detection of breast cancer. At this point, my own deepest allurement and God's gift of dominion and empowerment connected.

The passions I used to seduce women were now turned around. My passion was to help, to detect cancer early and save lives. All of this coming together—the allurement of the father's love, the allurement of a life work that had the dignity of the father's work—unleashed a tremendous energy and enthusiasm. Now I really was into pictures—healing pictures called mammograms.

I've been blessed by the expanding circles. In looking back I see how God was leading me and widening the circle. The many talking circles eventually led me back to my Catholic heritage. I've come back home to Mass. When we join our hands in a circle around the altar before receiving communion, I feel I am home with all the rest of the wounded ones needing the bread of life. I go out from Mass daily to join my team of technologists at work. We are one in Christ.

The more connected I become, the more connected creation seems. I'm hearing the birds sing and feeling the pull of beauty that is all around me. The circle keeps getting bigger and always more beautiful.

Like most pilgrims, Ron needed both psychic healing and direction from the Spirit. On the night before he died, Jesus gathered his friends together in what resembled a talking circle. In security and camaraderie they told their stories and then he surprised them. He left the center and washed their feet. He told them to do the same. He then went out from the security of that circle to face the chaos of the night. In all of this, he was moving in the direction of the Father's will.

Wider and Wider Circles

He drew a circle that shut me out,
Heretic, rebel, a thing to flout,
But love and I had the wit to win;
We drew a circle that took him in.

— Edward Markham, "Outwitted"

There are wide varieties of gatherings of new Americans that resemble talking and partnership circles. Ron's journey moved through many of them. There are many circles devoted to healing of some kind of addiction. Others are devoted to faith growth and outreach and bear names like RENEW, base communities, and Cursillo. Some circles, like Marriage Encounter, offer family support.

Common denominators emerge from talking circles. People interact in non-threatening ways and share with each other their life journeys. They discover that they are not odd or alone in their personal struggles with chaos and fragmentation.

After a parish talking circle had been together for two months, one participant remarked: "At one point or another, everyone said there was a period in their life when they did not sense the presence of God. It seems like we all have been Jonah in the whale at some stage of our journey."

The partnership of the circle helps Carl Hammer-schlag write in *The Dancing Healers* that " . . . each person must become one with the truth of his or her head, lips, and heart. If you say what you really mean, and you believe what you say, then you stay healthy."

IMAGINE: Think of a circle of people whom you could totally trust. What reflections would you bring to this partnership? What would you want to discuss to help you to "become one with the truth of [your] head, lips, and heart"?

JOURNAL: The circles I travel in heal because . . .
They do not heal because . . .

REFLECTION QUESTIONS:

1) "Spirituality is a way of looking deeper and discovering beauty all around. . . . " Where do you experience the most beauty in your usual week?

2) In an age of image making, the phrase "straight as an arrow" means to cut through the hype to the point. Can you think of friends who are "straight as an arrow"?

3) Black Elk, Pope John Paul I, Cesar Chavez, Rosa Parks, and Ron are people who if they came together would form a circle of wholeness and authenticity. What were some of the things they all had in common?

4) A talking circle would demand listening without interrupting, listening without contradicting. A talking circle would be a safe place where we could be ourselves without being judged. Do you need a talking circle? If so, why?

5) How might a talking circle help people to grow into more authentic persons?

2

THE
MEDICINE WHEEL

Now as I looked at the living creatures, I saw a
wheel upon the earth beside the living creatures,
one for each of the four of them . . . the wheels
rose along with them; for the spirit of the living
creatures was in the wheels.

— Ezekiel 1:15, 21

When the Rosetta stone was found in the late eigh-
teenth century, it provided the key to understanding the
hieroglyphic writing of the ancient Egyptians. The Native American medicine wheels are also Rosetta stones,
keys that give us access to the spirituality of the ancient
Americans. The circles of rocks laid out on the earth
have spokes of rocks leading to the hub. They are places
of healing energy and genuine beauty. They contain a
message for modern people. They are the prayer prints
of the Native American.

One such wheel is in the desert near Carefree, Arizona. Ironically it is folks with heavy cares who gather
there on this Saturday afternoon. They have brought
their brokenness and their need for healing to the circle. Most of them are in their twenties and thirties.

After a friendly potluck, they stand solemnly in a circle and undergo a preparatory purification ritual. A descendant of the Iroquois nation burns sage in a round shell and each participant wafts the sweet smoke around their temples and over their bodies. They then proceed to the circumference of the medicine wheel. Strips of colored cloth whip in the breeze signifying the four directions of the compass. The saguaro cactuses stand around the wheel, their barrel-muscled arms raised in silent prayer.

Through the years, the participants have witnessed oil spills, nuclear accidents, and food scares in their children's schools. In their families and neighborhoods they know relatives and friends ravaged by drugs. They worry about what kind of world is being bequeathed to their children. With a sense of disruption these new Americans come to this wheel seeking healing, seeking the spiritual wisdom of the Native American grandfathers and grandmothers.

Author Robert Johnson notes in his book *Inner Work* that "the self has characteristic symbols: the circle, the mandala . . . are . . . abstract figures that express the archetypal self."

Because of the powerful underlying symbolism of the medicine wheel the participants can enter it through imagination and intuition.

Sun Bear, who has led great Native American medicine wheel gatherings elsewhere in North America, explains how the medicine wheel helps humans reverence each other in the circle:

> We feel that each person has something to contribute to the wheel. No one has all the answers at great medicine ceremonies; we come together to share, to grow, and to help each person become

a more balanced human being (*The Shaman and the Medicine Wheel*).

On this particular day, near Carefree, the participants are asked to find their place around the wheel and to enter into a ritual of healing. One participant later described his experience this way:

> When my turn came, I laid down in a place of my choosing in the wheel. I was wrapped in blankets, like in a cocoon. In that dark place, my imagination intensified. I felt comfortable and secure. I knew I was surrounded by a circle of loving and caring persons. They then began to drum, chant, and dance around the circle. I could hear the sounds and even feel the vibrations in the earth as they danced around me. It was as though I was connected to a cosmic song. Their sounds were joined by the desert birds and creatures that lived around the circumference of the wheel. It was a strong participative ritual.

There are different versions of the medicine wheel, but there are some constants. By getting close to the basics and to the earth, we recognize in some way that we are all part of the whole. The symbolism of the wheel is in its connecting. Native Americans have always understood that. Buck Ghost Horse writes in *Red Nations Sacred Way* that "Since the beginnings of existence on this earth plane . . . native earth cultures called religious have used the circle with the inner cross as the symbol of life." Paul Steinmetz echoes this in *Meditations With Native Americans*: "The Indians' symbol is the circle, the hoop. Nature wants things to be round. The bodies of human beings and animals have no corners. With us the circle stands for togetherness."

The medicine wheel can speak to those gathered there in an intuitive way of their need to bring together the disparate parts of their inner lives and to live with paradox—the many living as one. It also reminds the participants of our need to be in harmony with the earth that they know is being poisoned. They know that humankind is destroying plant and animal species, that the ozone is being burned away, that climates are being altered, and that rain forests are being cut down. They see their own neighborhood and family circles being broken. They come to Carefree not carefree. They recognize brokenness and they bring their own experiences of brokenness to the circle. When brought together in the circle, this brokenness can coalesce into something new and beautiful.

Injured people bring fractured pieces to the circle forming a whole pattern. Perhaps the medicine wheel can be compared to the piecing together of a giant puzzle. As each part meshes with another, the beauty of wholeness begins to emerge. When young people gather at places like Carefree, they signal a growing awareness that it is precisely the broken ones who have something to teach the rest about the healing circle.

Expanding Circles

The medicine wheel is about harmony. Its symbolism can awaken our need to emerge from narrow ego concerns and to expand toward a more cosmic and holistic spirituality.

In the medicine wheel, people get closer to the earth. Through prayer and fasting, they become more humble. The medicine wheel is also out-of-doors beneath the sun. Dante hinted that we'll find no paradise until we find our place under the sun:

. . . I now beheld that glorious wheel,
Begin to move, rendering voice to voice
With harmony incomprehensible.

— *The Divine Comedy*

Beyond the sun, he saw the seraphim, and they too danced a circular dance!

Moving Circles

To experience harmony, we must join the circle dance; we must move off dead center. For Native Americans prayer is more than a head trip—it's a body and soul trip. They sing, dance, even run toward the circle. It's as though creation were a song and a dance, and each of us a note looking to find its rightful place. When we are in place, we experience a fulfillment—each of us a full round note in a completed score.

For the Catholic Christian, conversion and salvation occurs in the wheel—the faith community with the cross at its center. Our salvation involves an ongoing dance around the wheel. Salvation is not a pitched camp, not simply an "I'm saved" snug harbor. It is more of a run and a dance, a lively spinning of the circle whose energy is to bring more harmony "out there." It is ultimately not a "care-free dance," but rather a "freed to care dance."

The circle that dances around the spinning wheel can become for us an ever widening sphere of life, love, and service until that day when the Lord of the Dance returns in a new way to the center, and the Kingdom of God comes full circle. On that day Christ our life will appear and "creation itself will be set free from its bondage to decay and obtain the glorious liberty of the children of God" (Rom 8:21).

THE OLD AMERICAN

The gleaming rails of Union Pacific
are drawn knife point at the throat of the sun.
One exclaims, "We open the frontier!"
The other: "Iron rail divides the buffalo herd!"
     For one a passage to the sea,
     for the other, an iron chain.
The Old American was friend of the earth,
"The feet of the earth are my feet, the legs of the earth
my legs!"
The new builds towers, asphalts, and astro turfs;
When we think "dirt," we think detergents.
     The old lived in balance.
     The new out of kilter.
Time has passed; the iron rail still runs to the sea,
so does Love Canal...and eternal plastic.
Throughout the planet, missiles are buried,
daggers in mother's side.
     The Old American is silenced.
     The new begins to wonder.

A Symbolic Wheel

Four representatives from among Native Americans who are profiled here represent the four compass points of one gigantic, symbolic, North American medicine wheel. Each of these brings their own brokenness and afflictions to the wheel. They also bring their strengths and their ancient wisdom.

As we look back in time, a picture emerges. We can see how each of them brought healing and beauty to the North American continent in a holy way. They lived with beauty, and they lived beautifully. Their coming together in our symbolic medicine wheel creates a mandala of even greater beauty. Each life mirrors the diverse beauties of the north, south, east, and west.

The beauty of the north: Kateri Tekakwitha, coming from the land of wisdom, the buffalo, and the color white, brings the brokenness of an orphan and the handicap of partial blindness to the wheel. She offers us the white beauty of conversion, chastity, and discipleship.

The beauty of the south: Juan Diego, coming from the land of innocence, and the miracle of green in winter, brings the favor of the Virgin of Guadalupe. Like so many of the little ones in the gospels, Diego was a poor peasant, close to the earth like a field mouse.

The beauty of the east: From the direction of illumination, yellow light, and the soaring eagle, the founders of the League of the Iroquois, Hiawatha and Dekanawida, bring cooperation to the circle. Before the eagle was ever emblazoned on the United States seal, these two soared like eagles with their idea of democracy.

The beauty of the west: From the direction of the road of difficulties and the country of the black bear,

Chiefs Seathl and Joseph bring tears to the circle. They wept for what they saw coming in the future because of the greed of the white race.

These ancient ones form a beautiful pattern of wholeness and holiness—the circle. But looked at individually, they represent brokenness: poor eyesight, speech impediment, poverty, displacement. These are ragged edges.

The Lily of the Mohawks

Kateri Tekakwitha

...whoever would be great among you must be your servant.

— Matthew 20:26

St. Patrick's Cathedral, the Empire State Building, and Lady Liberty proclaim immigrant energy in New York City, while the woods, forests, and mountains of upper New York still tell the stories of the Native Americans. Long before the waves of immigrants built cathedrals, Native Americans worshipped the great spirit in this wild and beautiful country. As early as the seventeenth century early converts carved the cross from the virgin forests.

One of these is the most renowned and venerated of all Native American Christians. Her name is Kateri Tekakwitha, "The Lily of the Mohawks," a motherless child who drank the cup of suffering and gave her life to humble service. She who was a servant became great as the gospel promises.

Kateri was born in 1656 in what is today upstate New York. Her mother was an Algonquin Christian; her father a Mohawk warrior. At the age of four, she was orphaned when her parents and baby brother succumbed to smallpox. Kateri survived, but was left with scars and impaired eyesight.

According to Indian custom, she went to live with extended family, with an uncle who took her in. She had not been baptized, but she retained vivid memories of the religious stories her mother told her. By the streams, forests, and mountains, Kateri grew in age, grace, and wisdom.

Her childhood faith life was nourished by memories of her mother, her own personal prayer, and that which was of God in the lives of her people. Edmund Savilla writes that she went through a kind of Christian formation

> which involved an encounter with the lived faith of her mother, other Christians, and the traditional spirituality of her people. Today we would call this journey into self an intra-religious dialogue. A dialogue not only with the person of Jesus, but with the silent God expressed in her people's self-understanding. . . . Kateri's pre-Christian life is filled with many insights into her own life and the life of her people. As an active participant in the traditions of her people, she knew its truth. She would question abuses while affirming the spirit of truth expressed through tradition. Her vision would strengthen her sight, as she looked into the heart of matters (*Blessed Kateri Tekakwitha*, Tekakwitha Conference, Great Falls, Montana).

James Preston, a professor of anthropology at the State University of New York in Oneonta, has done extensive research on Kateri and Native American spirituality and understands why some of Kateri's early life experiences paved the way for her eventual acceptance of Christ:

> I think some Indians understand Jesus better than we do. They are closer to him because they understand suffering, because they are in touch with the earth, because they are humble. It has a lot to do with their sense of being a small part of

a cosmic whole (quoted in *St. Anthony Messenger*, July, 1987).

In 1674, Jesuit missionaries, called "black robes" by the Mohawks, founded a permanent mission in Kateri's village and established a catechumenate.

Kateri entered the catechumenate in the face of great opposition from her family and neighbors who were hostile to the white man's religion. Nonetheless, two years later on Easter Sunday, she was baptized. She took the name Kateri which was Iroquois for Catherine. (Tekakwitha meant "she who feels her way along.")

The journey of her people for eons helped prepare Kateri for her entrance into the faith. We know that Native American ancestors were living in North America 15,000 years B.C. We know very little about them, but we do know that they had religious rituals and belief in an afterlife. Kateri's story teaches us some profound truths about the spiritual tracks left upon the North American continent.

As time went on, the hostile pressure against her faith increased. Finally, in 1677, she undertook a long and dangerous journey north into Canada in order to practice her faith in exile.

As many handicapped people do, she developed her other senses and became adept at handicrafts. She was a combination of Martha and Mary—active and contemplative.

On Christmas Day, 1677, she received the eucharist for the first time. Most of the next three years were spent in prayer, penance, and the humble service of caring for the sick and elderly before her death in 1680 at the age of twenty-four.

In many ways Kateri's short life lived out the image of an arrow in a circle. Most of her life was lived within the circle of her family and her tribe. She was closely in tune with the native circle of nature: the mountains, forests, and streams.

The cross was in the center of her life circle. Kateri was orphaned at four, as a child her eyesight was damaged by smallpox, and as a young woman she was shunned by her community and she went into exile to practice her beliefs. The cross only drew her closer to Christ in prayer. When she died during Holy Week of 1680, her last words were: *"Iesos konoronkwa"*— "Jesus I love you."

Today, amid the hills, forests, and waters Kateri loved, she is remembered along with the Black Robes at the Shrine of the North American Martyrs in Auriesville, New York. She has been declared "blessed" by the Catholic church, a step on the way toward sainthood.

RCIA

Today the ancient catechumenate has been restored. Each year on the Third Sunday of Lent the catechumens undergo the first of the scrutinies. They are called before the assembly and receive a prayer of exorcism and then leave to continue their intensive preparation to receive the Easter sacraments. Like Kateri, these newcomers have been "in God" in many ways before entering the catechumenate. Grace has been at work in their lives even though they may have been unchurched as Kateri was for most of her life. Many are also making sacrifices to pursue this path; sometimes they even risk the disapproval of family and friends. Like Kateri, they do not take the sacraments for granted.

North America was fertile soil for the gospel, and for the arrow in the circle, but too often, the Indian culture and tradition has been considered "heathen," something to be obliterated.

Martin Marty writes that too often the white new-comers thought the Bible

> told them to claim dominion over the created world and to get the other peoples, the "heathen," to convert and yield to the will of the already saved. Given such impulses, they usually saw little incompatibility between the ideas of saving and enslaving the Indians (*American Indians and Christian Missions*).

The humble maiden of the Mohawks humbles us; her people's prayer tracks on the North American continent humble us. Like Kateri, today's catechumens humble us. They challenge cradle Catholics to respect the spiritual journey of those "outside the fold." Perhaps the yearly Lenten scrutinies should humble us too.

> You know that the rulers of the Gentiles lord it over them, and their great men exercise authority over them. It shall not be so among you; but whoever would be great among you must be your servant (Mt 20:25–27).

Kateri is among the first and the greatest on the North American continent.

IMAGINE: Kateri, half blind, making the 200-mile journey by canoe to Canada. Speak to her about your own faith journey.

JOURNAL: I am most a servant when . . .

Roses in Winter
Juan Diego

He has put down the mighty from their thrones,
and exalted those of low degree.

— Luke 1:52

North America has many different power centers.
Washington, D.C. and Ottawa are political power centers; New York and Los Angeles are communication
power centers; Chicago and Detroit are industrial power
centers. We recognize these immediately, but there is another power center, a spiritual one, that is likely less
familiar to us.

Pilgrims travel through a land of sharp contrasts
to reach it. Some go through lush green jungles, others cross arid land and rolling mountains. They travel
through sun-washed villages, past the adobe huts of the
poor, eventually to converge near Mexico City and the
shrine of Our Lady of Guadalupe—the spiritual power
center of North America for 450 years.

Consider why. After the Spanish conquest of Mexico, the native peoples lost everything—their autonomy,
their destiny, their gods. During this low point in a long
and proud history of the native peoples, a woman appeared to a peasant named Juan Diego. She was Indian;
she was dressed like an Indian goddess and clothed in
the sun. Something new was born at a moment of great
crisis, writes Richard Rohr.

Just when they thought it was all over, a new
"mestizo" Christianity unfolds. We are slowly . . .

54

learning that there is no other kind. Christ takes on the face of each people he loves. In this case, God knew that the face and features had to be feminine and compassionate. There was no other sign that could convert both the Spanish machismo and the matriarchal Indians at that time (*Our Lady of Guadalupe: Why the Story Fascinates*).

Because of this feminine symbol a whole native people was drawn to Christianity. In that image and story of Guadalupe there is spiritual power, but as is so often the case, this spiritual power is where we least expect to find it—with the poor.

The story of Guadalupe begins in the village of Tolpetlac near Mexico City where an Aztec boy named "He Who Speaks Like an Eagle" lived. When the Christian missionaries came from Spain, "He Who Speaks Like an Eagle" was baptized and took the name Juan Diego. On December 9, 1531, he was on his way before dawn to attend Mass in the village. Suddenly he heard birds singing like a choir at Mass. The hill nearby was covered with a brilliant white cloud and a human voice called his name. The clouds parted and there stood a beautiful lady dressed in the robes of an Aztec princess. Bright rays surrounded her so that it looked like she was standing in front of the sun.

She identified herself as the Mother of God and told Juan to take a message to the bishop. "A church must be built here where I can show my love to all of your people."

"But I am only a poor Indian farmer!" protested Juan. The lady replied there were others she could send, but Juan was her messenger.

The bishop responded to Juan's story with skepticism telling him to ask for a sign from the lady. Shortly after that, Juan's uncle became very sick with a fever.

Juan left to get the priest. On the way, the lady appeared again to him. He remembered to ask her for a sign. She told him to climb the hill and pick some of the roses he would find there. This seemed foolish since he knew no roses grew there in December. Nonetheless, he did what the lady asked.

At the top of the mountain he found roses as the lady had said. He picked some and put them in his cloak. When he brought them back, she arranged them in his cloak and told him to go and show them to the bishop. He visited the bishop and opened the cloak, spilling out the roses. The bishop dropped to his knees, staring not at the roses, but at the cloak. Imprinted on the course fabric was a beautiful image of the lady who appeared to Juan. The image showed Our Lady standing on the moon being held by an angel. Radiant sunbursts surrounded her.

Eventually the lady's request was honored. An adobe church was built, and until his death Juan lived in a hut next to it as the guardian of this holy image. Today, the cloak is venerated at the Basilica of Our Lady of Guadalupe. Juan's cloak was woven from cactus fiber which usually deteriorates in about ten years. The cloak is now over four hundred years old and shows no signs of corruption. Its colors remain bright.

Pilgrims going to this shrine come to holy ground, the earth that blossomed in wintertime. Before the white man ever came here, this was fertile ground to the native peoples, a spot they had dedicated to the Indian virgin, mother of the gods. Before the white man came, the native peoples had a spirituality of holy earth and beauty. They sang this song in 1490:

> From within the heavens they came,
> the beautiful flowers, the beautiful songs—

Friendship is a shower of precious flowers—
Let us enjoy, O Friends,
Here we can embrace—
No one here can do away
with the flowers and the songs,
they will endure in the house of the Giver of Life
(*The Poem of Ayocuan*).

Mary did not disdain to bring forth roses from "pagan ground." She, whose body was from earth, perhaps considers all earth holy. The Native Americans always have.

IMAGINE: Try to visualize the apparition of Our Lady of Guadalupe; pray the Magnificat (Lk 1:46–56).

JOURNAL: The broken humble ground in my life that could bring forth surprising roses is . . .

Rivers Flowing Together
Hiawatha and Dekanawida

Listen to me in silence, O coastlands; let the peoples renew their strength; let them approach, then let them speak; let us together draw near for judgment.

— Isaiah 41:1

By the shore of Gitche Gumee,
By the shining Big Sea Water,
At the doorway of his wigwam,
In the pleasant summer morning,
Hiawatha stood and waited.
All the air was full of freshness,
All the earth was bright and joyous . . .
— Henry Wadsworth Longfellow

In the land of Hiawatha, not too distant from where this Mohawk chief organized five Indian nations into the Iroquois Confederation, representatives from the four corners of the earth come together at the headquarters of the United Nations. For some, it is a "house of winds." For the less cynical, it is a gathering place for the nations that offers hope for our planet.

In some sense, the United Nations is an attempt to construct a fragile international medicine wheel. Its original dream following the cataclysm of World War II was to move from chaos toward cooperation.

That the United Nations should locate in this area seems only proper, for it is planted in the good soil of other leagues. New York was not only the home of the Iroquois Confederation, it was one of the original thirteen colonies to form the United States.

The Confederation

Dekanawida was a Huron, born in Ontario. He probably lived in the middle of the sixteenth century, perhaps earlier. He was a gifted leader, but he was also a severe stutterer. He was the mastermind of the Confederation, but because of his stutter, he relied on Hiawatha to be his spokesman.

Their efforts would create a union for peace and cooperation for the Oneida, Cayuga, Onondaga, Seneca, and Mohawk tribes. Because of this union, peaceful trading and intertribal cooperation flourished for a time among all the tribes scattered over upper New York.

The league was in many ways a beautiful model of democracy. As was Native American custom, there was always free and total debate. Once a vote was taken, bipartisanship, a dream in our time, was a reality in the league.

Moreover, almost five hundred years before suffragettes wrested the vote for women in the United States, grandmothers in the Iroquois Confederacy nominated the leading chiefs by secret ballot. They were also empowered to remove any male leaders who abused their positions. These grandmothers might well be a model for all women who deserve full dignity in the medicine wheel but who labor with the wounds of nonrecognition.

Virginia Armstrong writes in *I Have Spoken*:

> The Native Americans reverenced both mother earth and father sky. This proclivity to see nature in balance gave Dekanawida and Hiawatha fertile soil to plant one tree with many branches. Their reverence for mother earth also helped to form an enlightened view of the role of the feminine in bringing about harmony.

The beauty of the accomplishments of Dekanawida and Hiawatha is forever mirrored in their names. Dekanawida means "two rivers flowing together," prophetic of his life mission. Hiawatha means "he makes rivers," prophetic also. Dekanawida provided the dream, Hiawatha implemented it. Their working together and the creation of the league created a medicine wheel of cooperation and peaceful co-existence for previously warring tribes.

The league was formed as a defense against the encroachment of the Europeans and for nearly two hundred years it kept peace with the white race. Eventually the dream of Dekanawida and Hiawatha got enmeshed in the conflicts between the French and the English; later its loyalties were split between the British and the colonial revolutionaries which led to its decline after the American Revolution. Nonetheless, even today the league endures and the Iroquois issue their own passports recognized by the U.S. and Canada!

Today, when the United States Senate and House of Representatives gather by the shores of the Potomac and when the United Nations convenes on the banks of the East River, their coming together is fed by an ancient and honorable stream from "Two Rivers Flowing" and "He Makes Rivers."

IMAGINE: Dekanawida and Hiawatha standing before the United Nations and watching the various representatives streaming into it from around the world. Would they offer a blessing? What might they pray?

JOURNAL: The rivers that need to come together in my own relationships are. . .

From the Mountains, Mercy!

Seathl and Joseph

Be merciful, even as your Father is merciful.

— Luke 6:36

The Cascades rising up in the Pacific Northwest of America are mountains of tremendous beauty and energy. These snowy peaks were the last beacons for the weary pioneers coming up the Oregon Trail. For the Native Americans, they were, and still are, the last redoubts standing aloof beyond white man's conquest.

On Puget Sound, a lovely city hugs the inlets and hills. She peers west toward the orient and east toward Mount Rainier. Profound beauty and energy sparkle from this great mountain which Native Americans knew as *Tahoma*, "the mountain that was God."

Its aura brightens the nearby forests, the waters, and the beautiful city, capturing its sky and painting its skyline. So does the spirit of that city's namesake, Chief Seathl. His spirituality lives on in his words. They are an eloquent plea for peace and mercy. When visiting Seattle, one soon learns that this mountain sets the mood for the city. A day on which you can see Rainier is a pristine clear day. It means a break from rain and fog and a clear vision of her looming peak.

There is a sense of security about Rainier and her sister Cascades. There is also the looming energy of chaos. Most of the time, these mountains look like a ruffled carpet of green, purple, and snowy white spread from British Columbia to northern California. However, beneath this mantle simmers enormous explosive power. This is a young range, as mountains go, and it is capable of exuberance. Its many volcanic peaks are only napping. What might awaken was revealed in 1914 at Mount Lassen and in 1980 at Mount Saint Helens. For centuries the Native Americans lived in the shadows of Rainier and the Cascades, the holy mountains shaping the earth and the people. Living in the midst of such splendor many of the Native Americans had contemplative hearts shaped by earth's beauty. Two of the greatest in the northwest belonged to Seathl, chief of the Salish speaking tribes, and to Chief Joseph of the Nez Perce.

Seathl had a heart that was in tune with the great mountain. His name lives in a city; his spirit dwells in the mountains; his words reverberate wherever anyone loves the earth.

In his youth, he was a daring warrior, but later he converted from fury to mercy. After his association with Catholic missionaries, he became convinced that peace was preferable to war. Each evening and each morning, he would call his people to prayer. Out of his peaceful spirit came an eloquent plea for mercy toward the earth. He lived and spoke the words of Luke: "Be merciful, even as your Father is merciful" (6:36).

A man of peace, he refused to enmesh his people in the uprisings against the U.S. Army and spared them from some of the mistreatment that would ultimately result from the white man's greed.

Chief Seathl welcomed newly arrived white settlers. He was so well respected that in 1852, the new settlement near Mount Rainier was renamed Seattle.

Seathl spared his people from bloodshed. Yet, as a visionary, he could see ahead the mistreatment that was coming. He wrote an eloquent letter to the President of the United States asking for mercy for his beloved mountains, lakes, and forests, and for mother earth. It is as pertinent today as it was then:

Every part of this earth is sacred, every shining pine needle, every sandy shore, every mist in the dark woods, every clearing and humming insect is holy. The rocky crest, the juices of the meadow, the beasts and all the people, all belong to the same family.

Teach your children that the earth is our mother. Whatever befalls the earth befalls the children of the earth. The water's murmur is the voice of our father's father. We are part of the earth, and the earth is a part of us. The rivers are our brothers; they quench our thirst.

The perfumed flowers are our sisters. The air is precious. For all of us share the same breath. The wind that gave our grandparents breath also receives their last sigh. The wind gave our children the breath of life. This we know, the earth does not belong to us; we belong to the earth. This we know, all things are connected, like the blood which unites one family. All things are connected. Our God is the same God whose compassion is equal for all. For we did not weave the web of life; we are merely a strand in it. Whatever we do to the web, we do to ourselves.

Chief Joseph

Another great plea for mercy toward the earth and its peoples came from Chief Joseph of the Nez Perce. Near Yellowstone Park, at the 9000-foot promontory of Dead Indian Pass, there is a monument to this other mountain man with rock-like convictions. It marks the "road of difficulties" of Chief Joseph and his people as they were pursued by the United States Army one hundred years ago. Theirs was one of the bravest and most heroic trails ever blazed across North America. All Chief Joseph wanted was to remove his people from broken promises and expropriated homelands and find refuge in Canada.

If I could, I would take my heart out
and hand it to the great father—
and let the white people see that there
is nothing in it but kind feelings and love
    for him
and for them.

Those feelings were not reciprocated by some of the miners and land grabbers who encroached upon the heart of Chief Joseph's ancestral homeland in Oregon's Wallowa Valley.

When part of their tribe refused to be settled on a far away reservation, Chief Joseph led them on a heroic exodus. Their forced march would take them through the mountains of Idaho, through Yellowstone, into Montana. Along the way, their teepees were stormed in a dawn attack and men, women, and children were indiscriminately killed. Holding their own, and inflicting heavy losses on their pursuers, they slipped like vapors over snow swept mountain passes. Beyond Dead Indian Pass, in Montana, just short of Canada, they were surrounded by federal troops. In the freezing cold, they accepted surrender with a promise that they would be returned to their beloved northwest. Said Chief Joseph:

It is cold and we have no blankets. The little children are freezing to death. My people, some of them have run away to the hills and have no blankets, no food; no one knows where they are, perhaps freezing to death. I want time to look for my children and see how many of them I can find. Maybe I shall find them among the dead. Hear me my chiefs. I am tired; my heart is sick and sad. From where the sun now stands, I will fight no more forever.

The promises made to Chief Joseph were immediately broken. Like criminals, they were relocated to Fort Leavenworth, Kansas and then to Oklahoma. In that different climate, they were decimated by disease. In later years, only a remnant would be allowed to return to Oregon.

The pleas of Chief Seathl and Chief Joseph have proved to be prophetic for the plight of nature and of native peoples throughout the world. Examples abound. In Malaysia, nomadic peoples' survival is threatened by loggers. Five square miles of rain forest are cleared daily, the fastest deforestation in the world.

Seathl and Joseph, each in their own way, sought mercy for the land, the mountains, the forests, and the streams. Theirs was a "road of difficulties from the west." On their road, they left a message as lofty and enduring as their beloved mountains.

IMAGINE: Think of Mount Rainier, tranquil, snow capped, shining in beauty. Imagine Mount St. Helens, belching smoke, spewing lava, creating turbulence. Which mountain speaks to your life journey at this particular moment?

JOURNAL: Like Seathl and Joseph, I want to become more compassionate and merciful by . . .

JESUS, BE WITH US

Jesus—you are with us from Ring Around the Rosie
        till incense around the bier,
Jesus—lead us in the dance, circling, growing,
        merry-as-we-go-around!
Jesus—in our healing circles and medicine wheels,
        be at the center, making us whole.
Jesus—be with us in wedding rings and family circles,
        healing hugs, and sacred hosts!
Jesus—move us from dead center
        into the resurrection dance!
Jesus—empty the center; make room for the poor,
        point us out of self toward
           the wisdom of the north,
           the earthiness of the south,
           the insight of the west,
           the Easter light from the east.
Jesus—let us join in a circle, hand in hand —
        with the grandmothers and Lily of the Mohawks,
        the chiefs who prophesied and Juan Diego.
        Maranatha! Come! Lead us in the cosmic dance!

REFLECTION QUESTIONS:

1) To be in harmony with the earth circle would demand what changes in your own lifestyle?

2) In our symbolic medicine wheel, which of these persons is most appealing: Kateri, Juan Diego, Hiawatha and Dekanawida, Chiefs Seathl and Joseph? Why?

3) If Jesus Christ is the center of our circle, do we just look in toward the cross, or do we also look out for our whole planet?

4) "Are you saved?" is the looking-in question. What are some of the looking-out questions we need to be asking about the well-being of our planet?

3

WINTER'S DARK
AND HEARTH

Winds! all bless the Lord...
Fire and heat! bless the Lord...
Frost and cold! bless the Lord...
Ice and snow! bless the Lord...
Nights and days! bless the Lord...
— Daniel 3:65–66, 69–71 (JB)

Winter marks our passage through the dark. Outside, in the moonlight of a frozen night, winter's beauty sparkles from virgin snowflakes and mirror-smooth ice-clad ponds. Inside, the beauty of winter is found near the hearth of home. Around the fire are winter tales and winter wisdom. All the pent up energies of mother earth are covered over by winter's quilt so that they can brood and await spring's unfolding.

The moment that Jesus let go of life on a darkened afternoon, winter's icy grip on the soul was loosened and spring was close at hand. Compassion was being birthed from the dark womb of suffering.

The dark winter path opens into the light, but there is no light without the dark. Advent begins the movement through winter's gloom toward the solstice and the coming of the light that shines in the dark.

Out of our dark nights come visions and creativity. We begin with a heartbeat of life in the dark of the womb. We all have a shadow side, a source of tremendous energy. The Native Americans went into the dark on their vision quests. Jesus went into the darkness of the desert to confront the wilderness. When we seek the wisdom of the long winter's night, we plumb the depths. Rainer Maria Rilke writes:

> You darkness, that I come from,
> I love you more than all the fires that fence in the
>   world,
> for the fire makes a circle of light for everyone,
> and then no one outside learns of you.

> But the darkness pulls in everything:
> shapes and fires, animals and myself,
> how easily it gathers them!—powers and
>   people—

> and it is possible a great energy is moving near
>   me.
> I have faith in nights (*Selected Poems*).

The cold and dark of winter sometimes symbolizes sickness or loss. We all experience this shadowy path. Hope gives us our passage through such winter gloom. When we reflect on our difficult passages through the deep snowfields, we discover that the crises and the roadblocks had within them the possibilities for new trails. This is the beauty of winter wisdom: we have to live into the winter before we realize spring has come before, and will come again.

The Arctic Express

The Arctic Express is a loaded troop train that starts in the arctic switching yards. It gathers force and roars south. Its regiments fan out across North America. They carry battle flags emblazoned: "Wind Chill!," "Blizzard Warning!," and "Below Zero!" When they engage the tropic troops of warmth rushing up from the Gulf of Mexico, temperatures fall, rain turns to snow, and in the worst of winter's battles, whole cities are occupied and shut down. Humans hunker down with popcorn and rented videos in an eerie stillness punctuated only by the howling winds.

On blizzard nights humans get an inkling that they are not in perfect control. The capricious elements of nature are not to be mocked. A hearth-side wisdom says deep in our heart that we must huddle together and share the warmth of sister fire. To survive demands human solidarity. We are in something greater than ourselves and we are in it together. We need one another.

On such a January night, barely after the winds calmed and the runway was cleared of snow, a plane touched down at Omaha, Nebraska.

Tony and Mary Ann were there at the gate, awaiting the arrival of a Vietnamese family they were sponsoring. The plane taxied near the gate, but the elevator ramps were frozen and the passengers had to exit onto the runway and walk through the twelve-degree night to the reception area. When the Vietnamese family came down the steps, they were dressed in the flimsiest of clothes. They had been flying all day and they looked exhausted and confused. The last one to emerge was the oldest son. On his back he literally packed an ancient man whose cheeks were as wrinkled as an alligator billfold.

When Tony saw them coming, he grabbed an airline wheelchair and he and Mary Ann rushed out to greet the new arrivals. All that warmed that winter night were the smiles on that family's faces. Tony took inventory. One look at the old man, and he realized that he was dying.

He took the grandfather from the oldest son, put him in the wheelchair and rolled him toward their car. When Mary Ann brought the car around, Tony took one more look at the old man slumped before him and lifted him into the car.

Tony was right. The old man was at the edge of death. They sped directly to the hospital where his frail, dehydrated body was stripped, needled, pounded, and wired until the faint residue of life began to stir in him. By the barest of margins, he survived.

Tony was a successful businessman and he and Mary Ann spent days helping this tiny band get a foothold in a strange and frozen land. He relished using his acumen to get every benefit he thought they were entitled to. They had been loyal to us in Vietnam; Tony and Mary Ann would be loyal to them here.

The family would eventually move on toward the warmer gulf. Tony would finance a dilapidated fishing boat that they wanted. One son would work himself to death on that boat, but the rest would survive and prosper as hard-working citizens of a new land. It seems like there have always been families out in the cold, looking for an innkeeper to take them in.

Charlie and his partner, two Chicago policemen, were out on the streets on a similarly cold January night. They had been sent to check a disturbance between a prostitute and her pimp. When he and his partner got there, the only heat in the night were the curses crackling the frigid air. After breaking up their fight, they separated the pair and told them they were taking them in. Halfway down the dark alley, the prostitute said, "Hey, give me a moment..." He did, and a few moments later, she turned in the darkness and hurled human excrement at him. When Charlie told this story, years later, the listeners asked with disgust, "And what did you do . . . belt her?"

"No, I had my night stick but I didn't trust myself to use it, I was so mad. I just cuffed her and took her in." Compassion sometimes is not as easy as taking food to a family at Christmas, or caroling at a hospital. Sometimes it just means keeping a human spark alive in your own heart, in an icy alley when you could have hit someone with cold fury. Is the stronger man the one who channels his energy or the macho man who wreaks vengeance? Charlie's faith-work-spirituality passed winter's test. It is in the long working wintertime that we save our souls.

Don is an architect in San Francisco, one the media calls an "architect with a conscience." He designed homes for eight hundred Southeast Asian refugees and also homes that middle-income folks could afford in the high-priced bay area. "I wanted to build homes for those who otherwise could not afford a home. I wanted to give them a home they could buy for what they are now paying in rent." When Don saw the homeless sleeping on sidewalks in the midst of San Francisco's damp winter, he developed little "sleep shelters." The homeless liked them just fine, but the bureaucrats had them hauled away for "not meeting code" and left the people sleeping on the streets.

Pixie is a bank teller in Las Vegas. She really hates handling "all the dirty money." She also has painful varicose veins. Lots of "losers" come into the bank, sad and desperate. Others are retirees, "snow-birds" heading south for the winter and needing to cash a check. Rather than seeking the manager's approval most of the tellers say, "Sorry, it's bank policy— don't cash out-of-state checks." Every time they come to her window, Pixie makes the long walk back to the manager to seek approval. It's her daily "way of the cross," her own "spirituality of work."

Jessica lives in New York City and belongs to the single largest group of "working poor" in the country. She is a female single parent with children. When Jessica started to work, she joined 8.7 million single working mothers who were raising 16 million children.

She works long and hard and is paid less than a male counterpart. Wintertime means going to work in the dark, picking up her children from day care, and returning home in the dark.

Even if she could get on a more flexible career track for mothers that offered job-protected leaves, part-time work options, and at-home work arrangements, she would still be considered a second-class work citizen. Managers don't come out of the mommy track. Those who choose it usually signal the employer that they are on the B team. For Jessica, there is no hearthside fire without a long journey through the dark.

Winter's Wisdom

Winter sometimes tests us to the limits. Its bashing winds rattle our windows. In the north, its ice tests our balance. Its cold can measure our warmth. However, its ice in our face can cause our hearts to beat stronger. The words hearth and heart come from the same root.

Sometimes, we all have to journey deep into winter's woods before we find our way to hearth and fire:

My little horse must think it queer
To stop without a farmhouse near.

Between the woods and frozen lake
The darkest evening of the year. . . .

The woods are lovely, dark, and deep,
But I have promises to keep,
And miles to go before I sleep,
And miles to go before I sleep.

—Robert Frost
"Stopping by Woods on a Snowy Evening"

WINTER PRAYER

When winter blinds my eyes and numbs
    my hands,
Help me to see; allow me to feel
the outstretched hands of companions
tracking through the snow.

When I am deep in winter woods,
and short sun and long work
grey my moods and dull my senses,
let me see the starlight of one snowflake.

When work is done and light is gone,
with Sister Fire let me warm a room,
where stories are told
and my heart becomes a hearth.

Mountain Man

Winter Journey

No prophet is acceptable in his own country.

— Luke 4:24

Charred stumps stand as mute evidence of the fires above that swept through Yellowstone Park in the summer of 1988. There is also a fire below in the park—simmering volcanic heat below the surface that encounters sister water sending over two hundred geysers into the sky. The most famous spouts almost 200 feet into the air nearly every hour. It's a magnificent show, 10,000 gallons of water and steam roaring into the sky, holding the pose for about four minutes. Neither forest fires nor winter's ice get in her way. Every hour she proclaims: "I am Faithful!"

For many years, there was another "old faithful" out in Yellowstone — a pastor sometimes known as "White Rump Wapiti." That is because Father John Kirsch knew more about the White Rump Wapiti Elk than anyone around.

For many years, John was pastor to the parishes of Ennis and West Yellowstone where he later "retired." Each week, right into his seventies, John Kirsch would travel 150 miles between West Yellowstone and Ennis. Often, the snow would be seven or eight feet deep and the roads icy and treacherous. The temperature would often be below zero in this area that is one of the coldest in the continental U.S.

Father John was also "old faithful" to the waters, trees, and natural environments of the unique Yellowstone wilderness. He believed in a mystical way of seeing. To gaze lovingly at nature is more than just looking; it's the beginning of contemplation and meditation. He explains:

> All of nature is graced! We live in an awe-filled wonderland. Dualism is rampant when we try to separate God the creator from his creation. . . . The waters of this ecosystem, at base are filled with spiritual energy. The same spirit that allows Jesus to say, "I am living water." [You can]. . . become mystics of the universe, find the spirit within the material form, . . . be one with the cosmic dance at the core of all being!"

Because of this belief, Father John developed a retreat center in conjunction with the parish communities to benefit not only the parishioners but the many summer visitors to Yellowstone. He called it Living Waters Contemplative Center, a place where visitors would come to be guided on mountain "vision quests." It was an outdoor school for everyone, with nature as its text. He designed it to "develop an awareness of creation and the lessons which are hidden in every tree, rock, and blade of grass."

The trail that led John Kirsch through the wilderness to the "contemplative center" was a long one. After military service in World War II that took him to India, he returned with a dream to "go to the mountains." In 1951, he bought 500 acres in Montana and built his own log house. After almost a decade there, he was forced to sell because 500 acres was not a big enough ranch to make a living. This was a heavy blow. John felt his world was collapsing. This was a passage through grief, but also a challenge to move on. John decided to go to college and to graduate school to study the elk. He got little encouragement. He was told he was "too old" to start school. Despite this, John moved ahead, faithful to an evolving dream. He completed school and became one of the foremost elk biologists in the country. He was employed by the Montana Fish and Game Department and became deeply involved in ecological studies. In a small way, he began "mending relationships in the environment mainly broken by humans."

Mid-life brought a new chapter to John's life; he enrolled in the seminary taking with him a rich spirituality of creation. In the seminary his ecology and his theology converged. He was introduced to Teilhard de Chardin's *The Phenomenon of Man*. It connected with his life experience. He would always remember one professor who told him: "Remember—nature does not build on grace, but we live in an engraced nature."

After ordination, John taught for seven years at Carroll College in Helena, Montana, teaching the students eco-theology: "In my teaching I tried to eliminate the dualism between science and religion. After that, I formed core groups dedicated to creation spirituality in the parishes where I served." Those were days when awareness of the ecological crisis was faint and when such efforts were sometimes misunderstood. Some people were interested in eco-theology, many were indifferent and a few were even hostile to his efforts to make a synthesis between what he knew as a scientist and a mountain man, and what he knew as a man of God. John kept faithful to his dream. Soon, people were coming from as far away as Alaska and Arizona for vision quests. He so intrigued Barbara Walters that she interviewed him on network television and his work was featured in *Extension Magazine*, in April, 1985, his faithfulness the topic of an editorial:

> . . . Father loves his mission work. A life-long naturalist, he shares the miracle of God's creation and love with his parishioners and tourists. . . . The beauty of nature he says "cries out the glory of the creator . . . and leads us to care for and cherish our mother the earth and all her creatures." I thank the Lord for the gift of Father Kirsch. He has discovered a special way to communicate our Lord's love in this wilderness area, touching thousands of lives every year.

For many years, voices like John's cried in the wilderness — yet that is where visions so often stir.

There were many winter nights in West Yellowstone when howling snowstorms shut everything down. John would brush the ice off his beard, loosen his red suspenders, and kick off his mountain boots. Sitting by the fireplace, he would jot down his reflections, penning his hearthside wisdom.

Holy Water: " . . . it is in the wilderness that the salvation of the world is readied. For those who can see, all snow, all ice, all water is 'holy water.' At one time or another, almost all the great and little mystics have perceived and celebrated the presence of God in a natural setting."

A Healing Circle: "We moved to an open meadow and sat in a tight circle in silence and let the ancient ones (California redwoods) talk. There is much power in group awareness, especially in a sacred place."

Suffering: "Suffering is part and parcel of the birthing of the cosmos, and when suffering leads to birthing it is a blessing."

Violence: "I see violence as an integral part of the cosmos, terrible violence from which wonder emerges. It is only ruthless strife on lower levels of existence that gives humanity freedom to exercise mercy and gentleness on a higher plane. Mankind stands on the pinnacle of a predatory ecology."

Mystics: "Mystics will heal the greater Yellowstone ecosystem.... The mystic 'sees' and is filled with awe and compassion."

Graced Nature: "If we become mystics, we will see that nature is a sacrament of God's presence. We will learn the lessons hidden in every tree and rock; no one will rip-off a sacrament."

Cosmic Healing: "I must act as beautiful as I am, and you are! We have the power to heal the universe."

Aging: "The wear and tear of life is a constructive process, not a wasting one. It is a creative, evolutionary journey. We can upset creation by abuse instead of use. Human responsibility lies in relating. If we are selfish in human or earth relationships, the ecological balance is upset and nature begins to groan."

The Human Microcosm: "We need to let go of our fear of death in order to live out our vocation. The human preoccupation with escaping mortality grounds our ability to create and to let go. We would like to make the transition into eternal life by putting on an extra garment—a pullover on top of the rest, without any stripping or loss.... Yet, it is our destiny to be spent; obedient subjection to the wear and tear of life is a constructive process by which God can build up eternal life for us. The transformation of matter has already begun! We are all involved in a gradual becoming.... For the people close to the earth, the Native Americans, part of life is living with death. I say we cannot live until we let go of death. From 'letting go' comes new creation."

IMAGINE: Snow-covered Yellowstone, and the warm spray of Old Faithful rising in its midst. What does Old Faithful say to you about your own winter journey?

JOURNAL: For me, being faithful to my dream means . . .

Northern Natives
Arctic Wisdom

He sends forth his command to the earth;
  his word runs swiftly.
He gives snow like wool;
  he scatters hoarfrost like ashes.
He casts forth his ice like morsels;
  who can stand before his cold?

— Psalm 147:15–17

Sister Norita and Sister Joyce sit in the warm Arizona sun and talk about their days in Alaska, their smiles lit by the fires of the north country. The images they use send a chill down the spine.

The coldest we can remember was –74 degrees. Only the main community building at the orphanage was heated. Where we slept, there was no heat. So we wore winter clothes both when we were awake or asleep. Sometimes we would encounter a white-out while making the twelve-mile trip to the next village. Within a few seconds, a white curtain of ice crystals could fall around us. You just had to stop and wait. Eventually someone could come out for us. Like the son in the gospel, out on the road, we were lost and then we were found.

We learned so much from the Eskimo people. They had great warmth and faith. For them, love of family meant living for each other. We managed to find an old typewriter and typed out some basic prayers. Before leaving, we visited a lot of huts to say goodbye, and there hanging up on a nail would be one of the prayers.

No one lived alone. Everything and everybody was in one room. Each family might include uncles or aunts; everybody belonged to everybody. Yes, there was bitter cold, but no cold hearts nor loneliness!

We were surrounded by lots of wild game—bears, moose, and seals. One time, the hunters brought home some porcupine. Not one bit of it was wasted. The intestines were used for making thread, each quill was extracted and used for jewelry. The hide was made into mukluks and the rest eaten.

Their faith was simple and moving. They loved the rosary, the Way of the Cross, and the Mass. The Eskimo children would line the river banks to welcome father or sister. I remember young Johnny, a twelve-year-old; he came in from a distance for instruction. We gave him a whole set of prayers and he came back the next day knowing all of them. When we asked him how he learned them so quickly, he said he took them to bed with him and would peek at them through the night with a flashlight.

Perhaps their love for one another and their intense sense of community all came together at the time of a death. Everything would stop for a week. There would be prayer and story telling and dancing. Everyone was involved. The next child to be born would take the name of the deceased. Birth and death were closely related. The costs for any funeral were nothing. The men would make the coffin from drift wood. The sisters brought the muslin for the inside, others would add simple decorations. Favorite foods, a newly made blanket and moccasins were placed inside the coffin for the journey back to the source.

Because you couldn't dig in the frozen ground the bodies were kept until July. Even then, because of the perma-frost, only a two-foot-deep grave could be dug. This shallow grave was dug on a hill along a river. During the thaw, a wash down would occur and the ice would push the interred ones out into the current.

We were only seventy-five miles from Siberia, near the arctic circle, but in many ways, it was one of the warmest places we've ever been.

The missionary diocese of Fairbanks, Alaska, covers 409,849 square miles! The northernmost U.S. Catholic parish is there — St. Patrick's in Barrow. Here is found the Arctic National Wildlife Refuge. The only human settlement within it is Kaktovik, a community of 210 people on Barter Island surrounded by the Beaufort Sea which is frozen ten months of the year. At present, the only nearby technology is a Distant Early Warning station — part of the DEW line — its large rabbit ears cocked north and west toward Russia.

Despite its harshness, 1.5 million acres of the Arctic National Wildlife Refuge is home to hundreds of thousands of caribou, bears, a wide variety of furry animals, and 108 species of birds.

This is the twilight zone, the land of advent darkness. Its occupants, the Inupiat, are the twilight people. The sun sets here in November and does not return until January!

Unlike the people in the U.S. and Canada, the Inupiat don't worry about a perfect greeting-card Christmas or if they will receive a gift worth more than the one given. Just the family around the fire is enough to fill and warm the heart. Here the fears are much more elemental, like the fear of being frozen to death on the trail. Here there is a winter wisdom of what really counts.

Perhaps this kind of winter wisdom is what moved Sister Norita and Sister Joyce to say of the arctic: "It was one of the warmest places we've ever been. We can never forget the native peoples of the north!"

Spreading up around the top of the world, in the advent darkness, there are fascinating human beings. Everything about their lives is cold and frozen, except their hearts, their faith, and their love for one another. Around their fiery hearths is the beauty of winter wisdom.

IMAGINE: Think about what really counts in your own "winter waiting." Where is the warm place in your life?

JOURNAL: For me, to wait in joyful hope means that I must . . .

Silvertip Bill

Winter's Story

Mention the word bear and most men think of the stock market. Not Silvertip Bill. He's an engineer, a freelance movie photographer, and a lover of bears. That's why he signed on with National Geographic for a job that took him by plane, helicopter, tundra buggy, dog sled, and finally by snow shoes to Churchill in the arctic.

His journey took him over eighty-inch-deep snow fields and through freezing temperatures. It was a race to reach his destination by the time the water froze over and the polar bears started to lumber across to Churchill. Bill had a rendezvous, eyeball to eyeball with a polar bear.

The minute the water freezes over, there are bears everywhere. They come 700 miles to eat 400 pound seals. They know when its time and they know the way. When we got out on the ice, we spotted twenty-four bears a quarter of a mile away. I set up my camera and pointed it through the wide opening in our cage. When I used my rabbit call, twelve polars approached our position. I'm glad I'm an engineer because when the big one approached I could "guesstimate" whether he could poke his head through the opening of the cage and take off my head with a swipe of his enormous paws. He could not; his head-to-shoulder measurements were about three and a half feet. He came up nose to nose though, all 1000 pounds of him!

Why do I do it? I love bears and I love adventure. My first adventure was going into the woods as a child; my second was marrying my wife; a third was raising kids in the sixties. Bears are another part of that picture. I guess when that polar bear put his nose up to my camera, it was the same male inquisitiveness that I had as a child when I went out to the woods.

I learn from the bears. They don't waste energy like humans do on negative thinking and negative static. They apply their energy to the essentials. For some bears, winter means a kind of walking hibernation. Others, farther south, go into their caves for a long nap. They know when to come out and where to go. We could learn from them.

Coming Out of Hibernation

Not far from where Silvertip lives, men gathered at a retreat center to explore the male journey. Tim, a bundle of bursting male energy, moved and gestured and glared as though he was trying to rouse these men from their own winter sleep. His body language and his gestures seemed to say: "Come out of your caves! You've been hibernating too long!"

This was a mostly Catholic men's group and they were from all over the United States. Tim was challenging them to wake up to what their male spirituality might really be about. He told them that "the major parts of our male spiritual journey have been kept in cold storage! We spend most of our lives in the workplace and in bed. That is where most of us live out our faith and spirituality. Yet when do our prayers or the homilies we hear ever connect with our male sexual energy or our work?"

Heads nodded in agreement. These were men whose ages spanned twenty-six to seventy. They came together for a day labeled "For Men Only!" Before Tim ever got the floor, they had voiced their own male concerns.

They talked about being disconnected from their fathers and about deep father wounds. They didn't say that their fathers were bad, just that "they weren't there in their boyhoods," or "they just did not know how to be there."

They talked about cutthroat competition and dislocation due to corporate mergers. They talked about the need to keep their unique male energy while mellowing and changing, and owning their feelings as they moved through life's stages. They talked about the value of male friendships that were more than just functional but that were connected in deeper ways.

This retreat group was a first for most of the men, but not for all. Intrigued by the idea of linking spirituality and work, one corporate executive and three of his employees had been meeting during some lunch hours at work.

Tim expressed some strong opinions about why men don't link spirituality to their work:

> The reason why we do not connect our work and our sexuality with spirituality is because we've been led to believe that what is earthy is not holy. The farther away we get from the body or the earth, the holier we will be, and conversely, the closer we are to our bodies and to work, the less holy. That's how we get disconnected. The name for this disconnection is dualism. The opposite of dualism is connectedness. It is a both/and spirituality that says that both the body, and our sexuality, and our work can be holy!

Tim suggested three questions for work discernment: 1) Is my work eco-beautiful? Is the earth better or worse off because of my work? 2) Are my work relationships connecting or disruptive? 3) Can I tell my work story without shame? If I tell it truthfully, does it come out just? "These are pertinent questions about dualism and work. Dualism is at the root of all our separation and alienation!"

A thousand miles away, another men's group in an academic setting did something that is becoming more common. They started meeting weekly to search for the authentic key to unlock the door to a richer experience of their maleness. The black and female liberation movements had sensitized them and they wondered if humanity could ever be free while half of it—their half—remained frozen in old roles and expectations.

They described their male journey as one "out of rationalism and aloneness toward interconnection." They came to believe that individualism had unleashed many creative energies, but at a heavy price. Without losing individual initiative, they hoped to turn those energies toward more cooperative ventures.

Many miles and countless experiences separated these two groups of men, yet they were voicing many of the same themes and concerns. Some of the parallels: **Fairness**—*Men's group*: "Our work needs to connect us in a balanced way with creation and with other people."

Retreat group: "Remember when we were kids playing boys' games. The worst you could say to another kid was, 'you're not fair!' Where did we lose this?"

Male Energy—*Men's group*: "We need to claim our primal energies. The place where the wildman lives."

Retreat group: "As we mellow and become more open to our feelings, we still need to stay connected to our unique male energy. There is a wildman in all of us. The energy is there, but it has to be channelled . . . what's happening on TV and in the movies is the macho wild-man with no discipline or channelling."

Liberation—*Men's group*: "We need to break out of living just in our heads. The lonely long-distance runner symbolizes many men. He needs to enter the relays."

Retreat group: "As we get older, friends from youth become more important—if we can find them. They connect us to our roots."

Ritual—*Men's group*: "Every male until recent history was involved in some kind of male ritual. We need new ones."

Retreat group: When invited to put together a male prayer-ritual experience, this group did so, and talked about it long after.

Father Wounds—*Men's group*: "To be liberated, we needed to ritualize some bonding with our fathers, to bind up the father wounds."

Retreat group: "Some of us never knew our fathers. How can we know about the male journey when no male taught us as children?"

Life and Death—*Men's group*: "Grief—a fear of the loss of male potency—is a constant fear in men's lives. We don't want to lose power. Only when we deal with grief, can fear wane."

Retreat group: Ray, a vigorous, silver-haired Franciscan, asked the men if it wasn't "true that women are more connected in their relationships to the rhythm of life, to the life force? Look how much longer they live!" Most heads nodded yes. Some protested, "We do have a bonding with other men through our golf and fishing." Others were not so sure.

After all their discussion, the retreat group was sent off into the desert for some quiet time to make a "mini vision quest" to see what the wilds might have to say to their male journeys. At the end, they were given twenty minutes to put together their own ritual prayer service that would celebrate that journey.

They chose a song, a story, a poem, composed two prayers, and drew three pictures about the male journey. Their song was "Amazing Grace." Their poem, "Surprised by Evening" by Robert Bly, was of the night, and of seeing more than they may have been missing:

There is unknown dust that is near us,
Waves breaking on shores just over the hill,
Trees full of birds that we have never seen,
Nets drawn down with dark fish. . . .

The day shall never end, we think;
We have hair that seems born for the daylight.
But at last, the quiet waters of the night will rise,
And our skin shall see far off, as it does under
       water.

They entered the meditation chapel to the beat of one of their own drummers. Their prayers were about work and sexuality. They left to the beat of the drum, clasping hands firmly. The scripture story they chose? It turned out to be the story of someone who was lost in a winter sleep unto death, someone dormant in a cave.

They took turns reading sections until the text was finally handed to Tom, the senior man. With a deep masculine roar, he read, "Lazarus, come forth!"

He might have substituted, "Bill!" or "Ray!" or "Tim!" It was one of those days, a good day to come out of long winter hibernation.

IMAGINE: A liberated man—what would he look like? How would he act? How would he work? How long might he expect to live?

JOURNAL: For me, liberation occurs when . . .

Jeweled Markers of Our Path
Winter's Perseverence

...let us run with perseverance the race that is
set before us.

— Hebrews 12:1

Danita Begay Ryan reminds us of the wisdom we
receive from those who walk before us:

> As I look back on my Kinaalda ceremony, I have
> extremely vivid memories of the presence of my
> grandmother whose guidance and wisdom hold
> a special place in my heart. Her words of encour-
> agement and guidance during my ceremony...
> have become the jeweled markers of my life's
> pathways, and I will do my best to pass her
> words and example to my daughters ("Kinaalda,
> the Pathway to Navaho Womanhood").

The Kinaalda ceremony, the rite of passage for a young
Navaho woman contained a "running ritual." During
the sixteenth and final run from the door of her home,
she received her ceremonial blessing from the rising sun.
Down through the generations, this ceremony ritually
passed on the best and most heroic qualities of Navaho
womanhood.

Today's women are on the run. They too are descendants of heroic pioneer women. They inherit frontier
energy and they break new paths toward a brighter to-
morrow for all women.

You can see them on the streets of New York and
Boston, young women in running shoes, their dress

shoes in plastic bags, running through winter gloom toward well-lit board-of-directors meetings.

Out in the far corners of Alaska, women pastoral ministers and parish administrators break new paths, running from their snowmobiles to the warmth of huts where the native peoples await their visits.

Up in Montana, Joan reaches out a terribly scarred arm with the eucharist in her hand. She was making a long winter's run through sparsely settled ranch country when she had a serious accident. Her arm was almost completely severed. She prayed, "Lord, just let someone come along, and let me keep this hand so I can use it to serve you." Someone did come in time and her arm and hand were saved. Today, her hand reaches out with the eucharist. She drove incredibly long distances to take two years of training in a lay ministry training program.

Not only do women run through the winter, they also often have to hurdle great odds as they run toward the twenty-first century. One is chosen brigade commander at West Point; others go into space; at one time the four largest cities in Texas had women mayors. Each run sets up "jeweled markers of life's pathways" for those who follow.

There is also icy resistance, especially in the church. A bishop refuses to wash women's feet on Holy Thursday; a neighboring bishop obliges. A European cardinal wonders if it's wise to have women on marriage tribunals lest their "tender hearts play tricks on them."

Despite all odds, and all opposition, twentieth century women have run in the footsteps of their pioneer grandmothers; they have run so hard and come so far.

Who can forget Joan Benoit in the 1984 Olympics, running the marathon through the streets of Los Angeles, running through the dark tunnel, and then bursting out into the sunshine to the roar of 100,000 spectators?

Perhaps her run symbolizes the long struggle for equal dignity for all women. There is still a ways to go. Some women feel that they are in the long cold tunnel—in their culture, in the work world, in their church, and in their personal lives.

In the Kinaalda ceremony, the grandmothers play a prominent role. In all cultures, they are the marathon runners who have struggled the twenty-six miles. There is another grandmother in Oregon who has had enduring energy for the run, and who treasures the jeweled markers. In so many ways, she symbolizes the long distance runner.

In her seventies, Rae makes her cross-country ski runs over the snowfields surrounding beautiful Crater Lake. She is a woman of great physical and spiritual strength.

Sometimes people resemble their surroundings. It's that way with Rae. Her eyes mirror Crater Lake—a deep and vibrant blue. Like the lake that releases geothermal heat, they flash energy. Crater Lake's story is an energy story; so is Rae's.

Seventy-five years ago, she came into the world super-charged. She explains as grace her ability to leap the many hurdles of her seventy-five-year run.

I live in the present moment, but a medieval woman has shown me the way. My favorite quote is from Julian of Norwich: "I saw God in everything that is good and energizing. . . we are enveloped in love as bones in skin. . . and every manner of thing will be well."

My spirituality has developed over a long time. I've learned to say yes to the now. I gave birth to seven children, but I lost three of them in infancy. In his mid-life prime, my husband dropped dead of a heart attack. At age fifteen, my second daughter was diagnosed with Hodgkin's disease and was given five years to live. When she learned of the diagnosis, there was no "poor me" attitude. She came to me and wept and said, "Oh Mom...poor you! I feel so bad you will have to go through all of this with me."

Katy kept right on living in the now. Every summer, she worked at Disneyland. She kept going to school. She graduated from high school and went on to college. She attended Loretto Heights in Denver and pursued her English major. She was undaunted. She was even pinned to a cadet at the Air Force Academy. In her junior year, she was elected president of her class. She kept on living every day. At the end of her junior year, she died.

During those five years, I prayed the rosary every day asking that I would accept this as she did. I realized "Thy will be done" is either an acceptance or a lie.

You've asked me about the "jeweled markers on my life's pathway." Katy was one; so were all those other experiences of being a wife, mother, an employee, a widow, and now a grandmother.

Right now, I try to live fully every day. In the winter, I cross-country ski up by Crater Lake. It's an energy place where I get restored. I hope to get in shape to make a trip to Finland, and to cross-country ski in Lapland near the arctic circle.

Rae has eyes that have seen "jeweled markers on life's pathways." They sparkle like Crater Lake. From their energetic depths they seem to say, "All will be well. All will be well."

IMAGINE: Crater Lake. A perfect bowl of blue water surrounded by a rim of snowy mountains. Yet from its inner depths warm water bubbles up. Rest awhile by the living water.

JOURNAL: When my life's path is icy and treacherous, the jeweled markers that remind me that all will be well are . . .

WINTER SESTINA

(Adam asks of Eve, "Can I borrow your jacket?"
Much warmer and secure than this old leaf,
like the earth, it shows its vesture brown.)

It covers and nurtures like some woman
who carries a child across the floor
and offers the weary traveller bed and board.

She spreads a mighty feast upon the board,
hangs upon the peg the snow-flaked jacket,
and removes the droplets which slick the floor.
One more to eat means only another leaf
a place made welcome by woman,
the glare of snow, now a soft and amber brown.

Snug now beneath a downy brown,
the mattress tight against the board—
Last to go is woman
peeling off her cares like some jacket
and letting the day fall like a leaf
in a graceful motion to the floor.

The moon makes silent patterns on the floor.
All is still round the comforter that is brown.
Traced against the window pane, a leaf
that casts its shadow on the board.
Encompassed by the night, sleeps the woman,
the night, the room, the bed, like some primeval
jacket.

In restless dreams stirred within the woman,
closed in again and again with fences made of board,
tempted within to rise and pace the floor,

to cast away the leaf,
reaching for that primal jacket,
of earthiness, potent and brown.

> Put on the ancient jacket that is brown.
> Take off the leaf deadened into board.
> Emerge a diaphanous woman,
> more than a shadow on the floor.

REFLECTION QUESTIONS:

1) Which people do you identify with most? Tony and Mary Ann and the refugees? The architect? The Las Vegas bank teller? The working mom? Why?

2) John Kirsch, Silvertip Bill, and Rae are all energy people. What do you think is the source of their great energy? Think about some people you know who are like them. What do they say to you about an energetic attitude?

3) Describe some women who are jeweled markers of life's pathways for you.

4) What are some of the confining caves that men need to emerge from?

5) How do you react to the idea that "it is in the long working wintertime that we save our souls"?

4

SPRING'S HOLY WATER

Whoever drinks of the water that I shall give him
will never thirst; the water that I shall give him
will become in him a spring of water welling up
to eternal life.

— John 4:14

Joseph Campbell writes in *The Power of Myth*:

The Indians addressed all of life as a "thou." . . .
You can address anything as a "thou" and if you
do it, you can feel change in your own psychol-
ogy. The ego that sees a "thou" is not the same
ego that sees an "it."

When sister water is a thou, she speaks, and oh the
stories she can tell. She's come down from the glaciers
to form the inland seas. She's fertilized the Nile delta.
She's been the source of life to all the great civilizations.

She's splashed the feet of Jesus between the banks
of the Jordan. She's watered the horses of the Sioux and
was the settlers' companion on their long trek across
North America.

She has seen it all. Heraclitus, the ancient Greek

philosopher, stood by her side and mused: "River, always the same, yet always changing!"

If we look at her as a "thou," she will speak to us. Within her journey to the sea, we will discover the dynamics, the highs and lows, that are a part of our own human and spiritual journeys. She speaks in turbulent rapids and limpid pools, in waters falling and geysers rising, in dancing fountains and angry currents. She speaks to us in flowing and ebbing, in dying and rising. In billions of shimmering reflections, her sight is beautiful. In her rushing and swirling, in her cascading and splashing she sings the mellifluous song of creation. "Then he showed me the river of the water of life, bright as crystal, flowing from the throne of God and of the Lamb" (Rv 22:1).

In springtime, released from winter's cold hand, the waters of life do their own May dance, calling the birches and the meadows into green life.

Our springtime journey is with sister water too. Water is the church's great symbol of new life; the baptismal font the symbol of the church's womb. From it water brings forth new life in Christ.

Now we can look down from satellites and see our planet clothed in all its glory. We see white swirls and brown and green patches, but most of all, we see a beautiful blue. Our planet's surface is mostly water—precious and holy as the very womb of life, essential for the continuation of life.

Water is worthy of a loving and reverent relationship. To contemplate water is to "gaze lovingly." When Francis of Assisi gazed at water, he called her "Sister." Nikos Kazantzakis has Francis describe water in its simplest form as a revelation from God. When Brother Leo asked how God reveals himself, Francis responded "like a glass of cool water, Brother Leo, like a glass of cool water, cool water from the fountain of everlasting youth" (*What Is This Francis?*).

Native Americans have always considered creation as a "thou," to be addressed with awe and wonder.

In the arid southwest, the Zunis knew how precious water was and they listened to her voice:

> Running water, running water, herein
>   resounding,
> As on the clouds I am carried to the sky,
> Running water, running water, herein roaring,
> As on the clouds, I am carried to the sky.

> —*Mother Earth and Father Sky*, Marcia Keegan

In the heartland the plains Indians followed the buffalo herd through the lush prairie grasses and camped on the banks of the Platte river. The buffalo, the green grass, and the roaming Platte were all their relatives. When a thunderhead billowed up over the plains, it came as a friend bearing gifts. Black Elk explains that "when I looked on my people yonder, the cloud passed over, blessing them with friendly rain and stood in the east with a flaming rainbow over it" (*Black Elk Speaks*).

In the Bible, sister water speaks two languages, one old, one new. The language of water found in the Old Testament is usually the language of chaos and sometimes death. The great flood was a catastrophe; the exodus for the Hebrews meant life, but for the Egyptians, death.

In the New Testament water makes a great leap from a symbol of chaos to one of everlasting life. Jesus was baptized in the Jordan and walked on the Sea of Galilee.

The Woman at the Well

In springtime, the Cycle A series of readings for the Third Sunday of Lent puts Jesus at the well in Samaria, symbolically identifying water as a new creation, holistic, and healing.

In so many ways, this meeting at the well is our story too. Jesus has been out on life's roadways and has passed through inhospitable terrain — Samaria. Don't we each have our own Samarias? He is very tired and stressed as he sits by the well.

A woman approaches who is so much like the marginalized and abandoned of our day. Anyone who has gone through a painful divorce or who has suffered alienation can identify with her. Rejected, she cannot come for water early in the morning with the other women.

She and Jesus talk at the well, a symbol of life that plunges deep into subterranean darkness. The conversation that ensues goes even deeper. It is much more intimate than the usual gossip there. Jesus asks probing questions, perhaps embarrassing questions. She does not turn away—there is something about his manner—though she tries to change the subject. John's gospel paints a verbal picture rich in the symbol of water. Jesus does not stand in an accusatory posture. He sits at the circle of the well. He enters a talking circle and offers living water. In this whole scene, John has painted a picture rich in water symbolism.

He touches a wellspring and the life of new energy springs up for the woman, just as fresh water comes from the depths of the well.

"Sir, give me this water, that I may not thirst, nor come here to draw" (Jn 4:15) . . . .
So the woman left her water jar, and went away

into the city, and said to the people, "Come, see a man who told me all that I ever did. Can this be the Christ?" (Jn 4:28, 29).

At the Samaritan well, what is empty is filled; what is stained is washed. An alienated woman is transformed into a disciple. This water blessed by the presence of Jesus is holy and holistic.

This story of Jesus scrutinizing the Samaritan woman coincides with the rite of the catechumens who are preparing for Easter baptism. It speaks to their faith journey as they look forward to a fountain of living water at the Easter Vigil. At that vigil, the cross will be like a ripened tree on the banks of a flowing river!

In all of our lives, no matter where we live, somewhere near us, there is a river nourishing the tree of life. John tells us that "on either side of the river" there is "the tree of life with its twelve kinds of fruit" (Rv 22:2). Each river has a story to tell. The Nile tells us of Anthony and Cleopatra. Caesar crossed the Rubicon, Washington the Delaware. But the Jordan knows the Jesus story. When he stood in its waters, they spoke to him of a journey up the muddy banks, through the arid desert, and up to Jerusalem to a cross that would be plunged like an arrow into earth's side. Every river can tell a story that awakens ours. One such is the Platte — her springtime journey tumbles into ours.

The Journey of the Platte

In its springtime journey, it tumbles down the mountainsides through magic forests where wild deer and bears browse at its banks. It flows through a land of imagination and rich images. That springtime of life is where the first images of faith seeped deep down into our imaginations too.

Between the mountains and the plains, it passes through rapids, twists, and turns—its adolescence. For a while it even runs north, most unusual for a North American river. Do you remember your own adolescent rebellion?

Out on the plains it meets a mate where the North Platte and the South Platte, like a marriage, converge into one. Eastward is its journey now. Sometimes, there are dry years and as summer comes, the river seems to lose its career as much of it goes underground as a current in the great Ogalala aquifer. Isn't its disappearing act like the faith journey of a lot of young adults? Parents worry about their children's loss of faith. Those young adults may be like the Platte. On the surface they appear empty, but deep below, faith and living water flows. Sometimes, like the barren earth, lives are cracked open, so that the rains can come and seep down very deep. In other days, and in other places, these can well up from springs of living water.

Our human faith journey can be much like the river's journey, a gift from the mountains, twisting and turning over, sometimes out of sight, only to surface at a later time and a further place. Always, there is deep below the surface a gentle pull toward our source—our creator's love!

In eastern Nebraska, the Platte resurfaces and makes one last loop to the north—mid-life crisis? She then flows gracefully toward the Missouri, creating a garden in the fertile Platte Valley. When she embraces the Missouri, she dies, only to live a new life destined for the sea.

Not only is the river a symbol, its energy and our life energy are the same. Every springtime, the catechumens remind the rest of us of our faith journey. For most of us, our launching forth has not been so much like the catechumens' plunge into the Easter waters, as it is like the slow journey of the Platte. For all of us though, it is a journey out of the flowing baptismal waters. It is a river journey. Not only is the river a symbol, its energy and our life energy are the same!

Not so long ago, the plains Indians camped along the Platte, their dreams soothed by her murmurs. Their camps were always in a circle that spoke of their relatedness to creation. They left no toxic waste at the Platte, only faint and reverent tracks.

Today, a nuclear waste dump is placed near the great underground aquifer. If for some reason an underground aquifer were poisoned with radioactivity, it would remain toxic for millennia. Sister water still speaks: "Care for me, and I will care for your children. Poison me, and you abort the planet!"

If, like the Native Americans, we are still and reverent at the banks of any river, we might hear the prophet's voice echo over the waters: "Ho, every one who thirsts, come to the waters!" (Is 55:1).

IMAGINE: The Platte framed by a springtime sunset. Ducks bob in its gentle waters, sandhill cranes glide down to its shallows. Silhouetted against the sunset, they are figures out of pre-history. Hear their calls rising from the river like the litany "Holy! Holy! Holy!"

JOURNAL: Having begun my spiritual journey in the waters of baptism, how is my journey now like that of the Platte?

HOLY WATER

Holy Water, spring's exterior decorator, lay green car-
pets, wall to wall.

Holy Water of billowy clouds, paint a rainbow for winter's sorrows.

Holy Water, tumbling and falling toward the sea, teach
me the path of letting go and letting be.

Holy Water of my morning shower, sprinkle me and I
shall be purified.

Holy Water of morning's perking coffee, awaken me to
new day's delight.

Holy Water, my life's companion, speak to me of my
spiritual journey:

> I am dry and barren and in need of
> watering. . .
> My journey right now is over rough water. . .
> I am in deep water, almost over my head. . .
> I am bobbing along on calm waters. . .
> I am in prime time; each day like a plunge into
> refreshing waters. . .
> I am rowing hard against the tide. . .
> I am sailing beautifully, propelled by the
> wind. . .

Beauty of the Journey
Mary of Whiteriver

Think not that I have come to abolish the law and
the prophets; I have come not to abolish them but
to fulfill them.

— Matthew 5:17

North of Arizona's deserts the land rises toward a rocky
rim. Piney hills roll up toward the White Mountains har-
boring deer, elk, bears, and lions, plus much small game.
Here, the White River runs and the Apaches live.

The White River is well named. Its sparkling waters remain clear and alive with frisky trout. Here, young
Apaches fish as they always have. This is the last land
of the Native Americans to be surrendered to the white
man.

Long before the white man came, the Apaches lived
here according to their own law of harmony, an attitude
of being in balance with all creation, a law of kinship.
This law was ritualized in moving ceremonies, one of the
most powerful of which was the rite of passage for Indian girls from puberty to womanhood. From this ritual
some Apache women grew to prominence in their tribe.

The western Apache recognized some of the
stronger and influential women as "women
chiefs" .... The typical woman chief did not inherit her status, nor was she formally chosen. She
simply evolved into her role and gained recogni-
tion because she displayed wisdom and strength
and was a shining example of Apache womanhood .... She was expected to be most generous

in sharing her food and other material goods with those who were less fortunate.

— *Daughters of the Earth*, Carolyn Neithammer

Such a woman was Mary Riley. Her picture is proudly displayed at the Franciscan Mission in the town of Whiteriver. It shows Mary standing at the side of a young Apache maiden during her rite of passage. It shows a woman who lived the law of harmony, not only in this ritual, but also in her family and civic life. In the picture, Mary acts as the girl's chosen attendant. It was precisely here that the ancient law of harmony was ritualized.

According to Apache tradition, "White Painted Woman" taught this ritual to the Apaches, and it is she that the young girl will try to emulate. At the ceremony, a Shaman leads and is assisted by "Gan Dancers," impersonators of the mountain spirits. Spread out over four days, the rites are a combination of rituals and socializing. Because, in modern times, the Franciscan Friars have respected the cultural traditions of the Apaches, they have been invited to bless the grounds and the maidens.

Each girl dances and sings her passage into her life. She may dance four hours on Saturday and four hours on Sunday, singing some of the sacred songs. Each song is a prayer that tells a story.

In the evenings, the Gan Dancers arrive. Some, called Crown Dancers, wear elaborate fan-like headdresses. There is singing and drumming accompanying the dancing. As one Franciscan observes: "They know the power of prayer and spirit."

A girl who goes through such a rite knows she has been somewhere and that she is going somewhere. She has been touched by the cosmic dance. This is the deeper law, the law written in the setting and rising of the sun, in the seasons, and the journey of the trout in the sparkling White River. It is a law of caring and preserving, of sharing and of kinship.

Mary Riley participated in this rite both as a young girl and as the chosen sponsor of other young maidens. She took the law of harmony expressed in these rites and lived it out both as a mother and as a lawmaker on the tribal council.

On the steps of Saint Francis Church, in Whiteriver, the grandmothers sit in a circle and share years of Apache wisdom and memories. When they speak of Mary Riley, their eyes light up:

> She always smiled and loved everyone. She respected everyone. She fed the people when they were hungry and her door was always open to the stranger. The kids trusted her. She was "gomacha" (big grandmother) to the whole reservation. She loved the little ones—even the smallest crawling creatures. When we would go acorn hunting, we were afraid of the rattlesnakes, but she would pray them away. They would never bother us; they heard her praying.

From one of the granddaughters:

> Mary is like a patron saint; she told us the traditional stories and advised us. I now dream of her and wake up realizing she has blessed me. She talks to us in our dreams and gives us strong messages to keep our Catholic faith and our Apache way. She told us, "The Apaches had the cross long before Columbus came. We knew. The missionaries only brought the story in another language!"

Mary Riley was a Christmas gift to her family and her people. She was born at nearby Fort Apache on

December 24, 1908, before Arizona was a state. She always remembered her great-grandmother Aadiihe gathering the children around a campfire and passing on wisdom, "If you put your arms to work, everything you want is going to be at your fingertips." This was her first teaching on law and order.

Mary's father, a Mexican, ran a large dairy ranch and suggested that "someday you will be on the tribal council; I will teach you so that you will not be afraid to do things for your people." She wasn't. Mary did become a member of the council. She was the first woman elected to it and served for twenty years. One of her most important contributions was in helping bring the Fort Apache Timber Company to the reservation, which has provided employment for her people.

She also successfully supported the development of a recreation area that attracts thousands of vacationers to her beloved White River and White Mountains. In 1983, she was honored as an outstanding pioneer woman. In 1984, she received the "Spirit of Arizona Award," and in 1988, she was inducted into the Arizona Women's Hall of Fame which recognized her as "a special gift to all people."

Writing about her in the local newspaper after her death, Jo Baeza remembered her

> as an imposing woman . . . her confidence came not from any egotism, but from faith in her creator. . . . Mary loved the earth. She loved her mountains, and her family, but the greatest lesson I learned from her was that if people really want to get along . . . they can . . . no matter what the differences. "My father was Mexican and my mother Apache," she used to say, "if they could get along, I knew I could get along with anybody."

Long before any kind of women's movement was heard of in the wild White River country of Arizona, Mary Riley was a matriarch and tribal leader living out in her life the law of harmony. The White River is still living water flowing down the mountains; so is the memory of Mary Riley.

IMAGINE: An Apache standing at the front of the wickiup (tent) greeting the morning sun; see the green forested hills, the snow covered mountains, the clear flowing White River.

JOURNAL: For me in my daily life the law of harmony means. . .

Beauty of the Journey

Niagara and Letting Go

"Lord, how often shall my brother sin against me, and I forgive him? As many as seven times?" Jesus said to him, "I do not say to you seven times, but seventy times seven."
— Matthew 18:21–22

Old Faithful is water in all its beauty rising. Niagara is water falling and thundering. There, sister water, pushing and pulling, rising and falling, makes her way to the sea. On the American side the falls drop 193 feet; on the Canadian, 186. Here the waters speak with a roaring energy. Their mists hang like a bridal veil. No wonder that young couples in the throes of love honeymoon there.

At summer's full force, over 212,000 cubic feet of water take the long plunge over Niagara's precipice every second. In many paradoxical ways, Niagara Falls speaks to our life journeys. Her message is one of pushing and pulling and of the great mystery of letting go.

There is both a push and pull in the story of Niagara. When the glaciers retreated about 12,000 years ago, the land rose forming a dam. The waters pushed against the dam until it began to overflow, creating the Niagara escarpment. The journey of Niagara's waters began with a push out of the Great Lakes and they end with a pull of the Atlantic tides.

At the falls, the foaming waters let go and take their thunderous plunge. In this very letting go, power is unleashed. Both Canada and the U.S. derive tremendous hydroelectric energy from the falling waters.

Niagara's push and pull speak so much to our life journeys. Our passage from the womb is push and pull and letting go. So is the rest of our journey. Jack, who lives at Niagara Falls, can testify to these dynamics in his life story. He has experienced the pushing and pulling and letting go as gentle calls and forgiving graces.

My wife and I visited the falls on our honeymoon and then settled down to a good marriage and a middle-class existence. Seven years ago, I was a comfortable, uninvolved Catholic. Since then, I've been gently pulled and pushed into deeper waters. These have been little calls for me to share my gifts. I've answered those calls, grudgingly at first, only to discover later what blessings they were. When I say calls, I mean people around me challenging me to be generous with my gifts. This all started seven years ago when my daughter Erin made her first communion. She said, "Daddy, will you do one of the readings at my first communion Mass?" At first, I said no, but she begged, so how could I refuse? That simple event opened the door to many calls. After I did the reading, the assistant pastor invited me to be a lector. Later an invitation came to be a eucharistic minister and when I said yes to this experience, I was touched very deeply by the eucharistic presence.

Later, I was asked to substitute as a CCD teacher and that quickly turned into a regular task. All of these "yeses" meant letting go of my island Catholicity and launching out into the waters. I was amazed to discover that rather than being depleted through these commitments, I was energized.

The next call came from two friends who invited my wife and me to make a Cursillo retreat. I was thirty-eight and had never had an adult experience of Jesus. I was uncomfortable at first, and I kept asking myself, "What am I doing here?" That all changed on Saturday night when I made my chapel visit. I experienced an overwhelming peace and could feel the presence of Christ. The real presence was very apparent in this experience. When I left, I wondered what he wanted me to do next. My wife also had a similar experience on her Cursillo, so this was something we could share with each other.

I now was actively searching for more to do. I found it two years later. At a party, a friend invited me to work in Kairos, a prison-type Cursillo. My first reaction was skeptical and judgmental: "They deserve to be in prison." I was not ready to forgive one time, let alone seventy times seven! I would later encounter this attitude in many people when they learned that I was involved in prison ministry.

I made a very good ecumenical Kairos retreat. That weekend I fell in love with the prison apostolate. I saw sixty prisoners, really almost kids, in prison green and twenty team members in their midst. At the closing, two hundred others gathered outside the prison gates, with lighted candles. I came away from that retreat realizing that those prisoners were in desperate need of Christ's love. Most of them had never experienced unconditional love in any fashion.

Since that retreat, I have spent every Friday night in prison visitation and follow-up. During that time, I became aware of their many religious needs and I expressed these to the chaplain. He answered, "Are you available?"

I said, "For what?"

"For anything!" he answered. "There is no RCIA program for the prisoners and since I cover two prisons, I can't start one. How about you?" Another call!

With some training from the chaplain and a nun I started an RCIA program. I was excited. Fifty men signed up but only nine came to the first session. That taught me a little humility and challenged me. I was now doing visitation on Friday evenings and the RCIA on Saturday afternoons. This prison ministry had turned into something very special. One prisoner was especially slow to respond and asked me with a very puzzled expression, "Why do you come?"

I answered, "I grow spiritually because of you guys." It's true I feel a call to them; whether explaining the faith to Bob, who can't read, or teaching John to say the rosary, I'm energized. Some of our friends cannot understand this. "Cons are to be shunned and isolated," they say. But I think the Spirit calls us to bring love into that isolation. Thank God for my wife and two daughters who understand what I am trying to do and support it completely.

When I was programmed into the macho thing, feelings of compassion made me feel uncomfortable. Now, I realize my compassion is an asset. I think I am beginning to grow up spiritually with the prisoners helping me. For whatever help I have given them, I have received back a thousandfold. It's amazing, I hate my eighty-mile round trip drive to work, yet the drive to the prison never seems long.

Recently, I was invited to go on a retreat. On the first day I said to the Lord, "I just can't stand the daily grind of that eighty-mile drive but I have to let this into your hands Lord. I have to let go of my anxiety and trust your way for me." The next morning, there was a message at the retreat desk to call my employer. When I reached him he told me I'd been promoted, given a raise and reassigned to Niagara Falls. That means thirty miles less driving for me every day. Yes, I've been pushed and pulled. I believe it is the dynamics of grace—surprising, unexpected grace. I could only give myself to the prison ministry because of the love and support I receive from my wife and two daughters. I met my wife in the third grade! Our marriage is wonderful because we support each other's spiritual life. We grew up as kids together, now I think we are growing up together spiritually. Recently, a priest asked me to give some thought to the diaconate. I will, but I have to make sure it is what God wants for me and for others.

We live close to the falls and I love their powerful energy, but I would have to say that some of the most energizing and fulfilling moments of my life have been experienced behind prison walls. My sharing Jesus Christ with the prisoners and their sharing the Lord with me have given me more and more glimpses of God's love that I could have never found elsewhere.

IMAGINE: Niagara Falls thundering over the precipice, letting go, dropping, foaming, forming a curtain of mist as it hits the river below. Feel its spray; look down and glimpse a rainbow in its mists.

JOURNAL: In my own letting go, God may be gently pulling me toward . . .

Beauty of the Journey
Women at the Well

> I slept by the wall of the courtyard, and my face
> was uncovered. I did not know that there were
> sparrows on the wall and their fresh droppings
> fell into my open eyes and white films formed
> on my eyes.
>
> — Tobit 2:9–10

There is a spiritual path we all experience. It might well be called the messy path. Ask Tobit about it! He goes outside and bird droppings blind his eyes.

Families, neighborhoods, work places can all be messy. If we observe closely, all systems and all groups are somewhat dysfunctional—messy to some degree. Sometimes we are tempted to think, "If I could just get out of this mess and get over there, then everything would be okay." But "over there" will likely be another mess.

We can never evade all the little messes in life. Our challenge is to clean up the little messes and move on. Living with some mess is called living with paradox. However, there are too many other messes that are intolerable. With those, we have to get out, get organized, or get help. The following stories are about two women who have dealt with intolerable messes.

Anastasia

Hispanics are the fastest growing ethnic group in the United States. Many encounter the same obstacles placed against earlier ethnic groups who came to the U.S. Often, they must struggle for what others take for granted. In some border communities, many live without water or sewer systems. This story is about one woman who sought a way out of such a mess, a woman at the well seeking living water.

Anastasia came from a background of extreme poverty. A middle child in a family of eight she left the first grade to begin working. She delivered groceries and always asked if she could have the paper that wrapped the meat. She used this precious paper to practice her writing skills. Throughout her youth, she worked to help support her family.

After she grew up and married Frank, they lived in the inner city where their child was born. They had to raise Frank Junior in a terrible mess—in the midst of the pressure of gangs and drugs. They wanted more for their son. When he became a teenager and earned his black belt in karate they were very proud of what he had done through self-discipline and concentration.They very much wanted to move out of the inner city so they scrimped and saved and eventually were able to buy a parcel of land on the outskirts of town. Many other Hispanics also scrimped and saved to buy property and move to the same area. Soon it was a suburb, but with a difference. It lacked basic services like water, sewers, and decent roads.

When no services were forthcoming, Anastasia was invited to join an inter-religious community organizing group called EPISCO and through it things began to move off center. The group became effective enough to get the attention of a national newsmagazine.

Anastasia became one of its leaders and now has a community identity.

I believe in EPISCO. We are EPISCO. Through EPISCO, we learn how to work with others for water, roads, sewage, and services. EPISCO teaches us how to work for ourselves. How do we keep going? We keep faith in God and in ourselves. Faith and hope are sisters! We are the only ones who can speak for the benefit of our children. We must do so. In so many ways, we have so very little, but in family and community, we are rich. We believe that with God, all is possible!

With intolerable messes, you have to get out, get organized, and get healed!

Marcia

It is not an enemy who taunts me—then I could bear it; it is not an adversary who deals insolently with me—then I could hide from him. But it is you, my equal, my companion, my familiar friend.

— Psalm 55:12–13

Marcia is another woman seeking life-giving waters. She is also growing out of early childhood abuse. A counselor who has seen hundreds of women through the years says that sexual and other violent types of abuse of women are the unfolding stories of our time: "Marcia's experience is just the tip of the iceberg!" Joyce Hollyday wrote that

In a Cosmopolitan survey of 160,000 women, 24 percent have been raped at least once. According to Nancy Gage and Cathleen Schurr in *Sexual Assault* between 300,000 and 1.1 million women are raped each year. The FBI estimates that if current trends continue, one in four women will be sexually assaulted in her lifetime.

— "An Epidemic of Violence," *Sojourners*

Marcia is not yet fifty. She wears a wide brimmed hat that frames her black hair flecked with grey. She is strikingly attractive. Her face is calm. There are no wrinkles to hint of any cares. You might speculate her age at thirty-five. Her green eyes are peaceful. She is articulate and intelligent and speaks from a firm grounding of inner peace. But it has not always been so. For a long time, she traveled a messy path.

When I was conceived, neither of my parents were ready. My father needed a son to boost his ego. My mother wanted a career. It's almost like I sensed that in the womb, as though I decided not to be born. I turned my back on birth. My mother required a caesarean, and both of us almost died. I was kind of born in spite of myself.

At age two and one half, my father molested me. When my mother walked in on us, he threatened to kill her, and tried to. We moved away and I have seen him only a couple of times since then. My mother remarried. My stepfather was an alcoholic and a wife beater. He was even convicted but she would always take him back. My mother never went to church but she did send us to Sunday school. At sixteen, I stopped saying the creed because I didn't believe any more. . . and yet, I always was searching.

Ten days after graduation from high school, I married just to get out of the house. The marriage lasted eight years and was followed by two others. These were years of depression and unhappiness, also years of moving about, even as far as Europe.

Through my young adulthood, I kept on searching for the "real." I was into everything, sampling many churches. At forty-one, I began to sense a pattern in my relationships with men. I realized that I tended to date men who hated women! I talked to a female counselor, and she asked me if I was ever molested. "You exhibit the classic symptoms," she explained.

Later, I was invited to a weekend retreat. At first, I was put off. I have always been very rational and any showing of emotion in prayer did not attract me. I was very much tempted to leave, but I decided to stay on. At the closing session on Sunday, I was encircled by people who were praying and I asked them to pray with me so that I could forgive my father. I felt a difference and my life has not been the same since.

One day, while sitting next to a lake and reading the Twenty-third Psalm, I experienced an incredible joy. "He leads me beside still waters; he restores my soul." These words came alive for me.

After that, I began to have even more contact with church communities. Perhaps one of the most important spiritual contacts I made was at work! I had a boss who conducted a six-week Bible course during lunch hour at the agency. It was just calm discussion, nothing spectacular. At the end, we were encouraged to ask God for a special gift. I asked to see reality as it is, not just the way I want it to be. Since then, prayer entered my spiritual house and has stripped away all the accumulated layers of messy varnish and paint.

Shortly after that, I moved to the sunbelt where I had been promised a job paying $7,000 monthly. Chaos intervened. The job had been misrepresented and I was without steady income. I owed taxes to the foreign country I had lived in and planned to pay them with the money from my new job. Then when I finally did start earning some money it was garnisheed. I was living in a glitzy paradise and wondered, "How can it look so good and be so bad?" My prayer to see the "real" was beginning to be answered.

I was living on Isaiah 41, but had no church community. One day, I woke up and knew I had to fast and pray and find a church. On my own, I started to go to daily Mass. After three months of this, I met a priest who mentioned the RCIA. I found the rituals of the RCIA very powerful. The signing with the cross fit my journey. The scrutinies stirred up my quest for the real. I even stopped tinting my hair! I was tired of creating illusions about myself. At Easter, I was received into the Catholic church. The story all neatly wrapped up? Not at all. A few weeks after Easter, I went to Vegas and entered a civil marriage that lasted for all of three months.

The next time I went to church, the priest opened his homily by saying, "Some people want to be loved so badly they opt for the counterfeit rather than the real." More than ever I longed for the real. I went to a retreat house, was recommended to a spiritual director who asked if I was ever molested. He helped me realize that as a result of that early incident my life was one of delusions. "You attract people who hate women and your desire to please and make up brings you more burdens. You deceive yourself and others."

Once again my prayer to see reality as it is was being answered. Layer by layer, deceit was being peeled away. This spiritual direction gave

SEASONS OF THE EARTH AND HEART

me a new way through the garbage. Since then, I have even thanked God for chaos because having told my story, I can now listen to others.

What you see is a miracle. At one point I was down to fifty cents in my pocket. I walked across the parking lot asking God, "What am I going to do?" At my car door I found a twenty-dollar bill.

I go to Mass and communion daily; my friends who know my story cannot figure out how I can be so peaceful and joyful. It is because I now know that God was with me all the time on the messy paths. My spiritual task was to come to grips with illusions. I didn't trust anybody because my parents were unable to teach me to trust. I can now look back and discover the grace that has seen me through my chaotic journey.

I now live by the side of a creek. I love the beauty of it, but mostly, I love the beauty I am experiencing in my spiritual life, the joy and peace of being with the Lord next to living waters.

IMAGINE: You and the Lord next to the waters. Are they calm? Are they turbulent? What do you need to say to the Lord there?

JOURNAL: Sometimes we are tempted to think, "If I could just get out of this mess and get over there, then everything would be okay." But there is probably a different mess over there. Our challenge is to clean up little messes in our lives and move on. However, there are sometimes intolerable messes that demand we get organized, get help, or get out. Right now, in my own messiness, I need . . .

Beauty of the Journey

The Catechumens

When the poor and needy seek water, and there
is none, and their tongue is parched with thirst,
I the Lord will answer them, I the God of Israel
will not forsake them. I will open rivers on the
bare heights, and fountains in the midst of the
valleys.

— Isaiah 41:17–18

Pat is twenty-eight years old and a mobile North American. She has lived on the west coast, the gulf coast, and in the desert. She is fresh from the Easter waters, baptized at a recent Easter Vigil.

Although her grandfather was a minister, she and her brothers and sisters were not brought up in any church. As a child, she experienced the warmth and devotion of some kind Baptist neighbors. Between ages four and ten, she went to church with them and it was a good place for her to be. But when the family moved to a rural area she was not comfortable at the nearby church. "It was so different from the Baptist church of my early childhood—all fire and brimstone and no love." Like most spiritual journeys, hers has been a winding stream.

My childhood was not normal. I worked
ever since I was eleven and my mother was not
well and was hospitalized a lot. My father tended
to be violent especially when under pressure. In
1980, he was killed in an auto accident.

I had a lot of responsibility and experienced
a lot of pressure caring for my brothers and

126

sisters. I seemed to become obsessive about work. During this time I also had four abortions. I seemed to be in a fog—my mother in the hospital and me a teenager running the house. Like a lot of young people, I also got into drugs. In every way I was in over my head.

Then I was seriously injured in a car accident. During the recuperation, I at last had permission "not to work" and I began to think about my life. I realized I was a very creative person and wondered why I was abusing my talents and myself.

I had also attended a seminar on anger and it was a revelation to learn what had been going on inside me.

I eventually married and I started praying for a new life, praying that we could be who we really are, praying to get out of our old life. After awhile my husband and I both decided to drop out of our circle of friends. My husband had been raised a Catholic and we decided to go to Christmas Mass. Warmed by the experience, we started going to weekly Mass.

Eventually, I was invited to participate in the RCIA. I liked it. The small groups allowed me to open up slowly. It just went on in gradual stages. When it came time to decide to be baptized I got nervous. I felt unworthy because of my past life.

But I went ahead. The RCIA rituals turned out to be powerful spiritual experiences. I'll never forget being enrolled and having the sign of the cross traced on me. And on Holy Thursday, my sponsor washed my feet. I was touched so deeply that my sponsor would get on her knees in prayer and service for me. It actually took away my shame. I realized Jesus is here. I can't be ashamed. He has loved me too much for that.

During that Lent, on the way to Easter, I fasted and lost thirty pounds. I was actually being good to my body, not abusing it as I had in the past. At some point during that Lent, I began to be drawn toward baptism instead of being pulled back to shame.

My experience of baptism was joyous. I did not try to analyze it. I just went with it and I came out of the water feeling free and lifted up.

You know what? I wanted to have a baby, but could not get pregnant. On the way to baptism, I did! Moving toward a new life . . . we were given a new life!

Pat told her story as she held her two-and-a-half-month-old baby son in her arms.

At the Easter Vigil when Pat was baptized, there were thirty other adults in her group. One of them was Mark. He is a handsome, suntanned thirty-year-old. He tells his story next to his pickup truck and his handsome Irish setter:

I guess my Easter story is about coming to God. I've had lots of problems. I always believed I could solve my own problems, but I reached a point one day when I realized I needed help. I was doing drugs and my lifestyle was destructive. I finally reached a point where I was in trouble with the law and could have gone to prison. One day, I started to cry in the presence of my employer. Out of that crisis came a friendship.

The couple who employed me eventually invited me to church with them. I saw the catechumens being dismissed during the Lenten Masses, and I decided I wanted to be among them. My employer became my sponsor. I was baptized at Easter; I had a feeling of belonging, of being supported. God drew me to baptism through my sponsor and other good people. As I look back, God seemed to send key people into my life at crucial moments.

Mark reached down and petted the setter's head. "Beautiful story, huh!"

In every diocese, there are hundreds of newcomers received into the church each Easter. Through the RCIA they have shared their stories with each other and discovered from that that God was with them in their journeys. At the vigil, the Exodus story of how God was with the Hebrew people on their journey through the Red Sea resonated with their own spiritual journeys.

For Pat and Mark and so many others, the beauty of spring will always remind them of a passage through the holy waters to even greater beauty.

IMAGINE: The catechumens coming out of the Easter waters, smiling, some crying tears of joy. Remember some tears of your own and how you passed through those tears.

JOURNAL: As I look back, I can discover God and amazing grace being with me even in the twists and turns of my life journey. I especially remember . . .

REFLECTION QUESTIONS:

1) Reflect on some happy memories you have of experiences with water—fishing, swimming, boating, even playing with a hose as a kid on a hot summer day.

2) Where are you in your personal spiritual journey in comparison to the journey of the Platte River? Are you in rough rapids? running north against the odds? disappearing underground?

3) How has your life been messy? Do you need to get out, get organized, or get help?

4) Every spring the catechumens go into the waters of baptism and emerge cleansed for a new life. Have you had similar passages?

5

SUMMER'S
HEALING EARTH

God called the dry land Earth, and the waters
that were gathered together he called Seas. And
God saw that it was good.

— Genesis 1:10

Summertime is earth time. We flee the cities and travel
over the green-clad land seeking beauty and recreation.
Even in cities we find a bit of earth wherever we can—a
park, a ballfield, a plot of earth in the yard for vegetables,
even a windowbox or flowerpot.

In the summer we are reminded to touch the earth,
and when we do, we rediscover our roots. We begin to
realize that we have been formed and shaped by mother
earth. We are awakened to an awareness that our destiny
and the earth are connected.

Travelers to the Holy Land are often more impressed by the outside places than they are by the ancient buildings. These are much the same as they were
in the time of Jesus. They speak about him and remind
pilgrims that we are all shaped by the land where we
live, just as Jesus was formed by the desert, the Jordan,
the wilds of Samaria, the fertile hills of Galilee, and the

blue sea. These places shaped his body, his imagination, and his words.

The Beatitudes were spoken from a fertile oasis surrounded by a forbidding wilderness. Jesus could speak them because he had experienced an oasis in the center of harshness. "Blessed are the poor in spirit for the Kingdom of heaven is theirs"—the poor in the desert of loss can experience the oasis of blessing. "Blessed are the lowly for they shall inherit the earth"—those who walk through the desert of failure can reach the oasis of new beginning. The people were drawn to Jesus because he spoke out of their experience in their own land. He used the language of their earth to speak of the mystery of God: in barren Samaria, he promised a well of living water; beside the fertile vineyards of Galilee, he identified himself as the true vine.

Mother earth has always been both a benefactor and a teacher. When the first explorers crossed the plains, they called them the "Great American Desert." Yet, hidden a few feet below the surface is one of the largest sources of water on our continent—the Ogalala aquifer. The settlers eventually tapped this hidden resource and turned the desert into a garden and were shaped by both.

Mother earth gave the bison-filled plains to the Native Americans. She provided the oil-rich plains of Texas, the wheat fields of Alberta, the game-rich lakes and woods of Ontario, the silver mountains of Nevada. In her seasonal rhythms she teaches us a time to plant and a time to reap, a time to conserve, and a time to let go.

She speaks to us from all the byways that cross her—the settlers' wagon-rutted trails, the roads of the conquistadors, and the paths of the trappers.

Long before the pilgrims gave thanks for the land, the Native Americans lived in harmony with North American earth, gratefully receiving her benefits, and carefully listening to her teaching. They cherished and blessed the land. Their ancient experience of the land as a holy place of prayer should not be blotted from our memories. In some God-given and mysterious way, those who have gone before us are a part of who we are. Their journey and the earth that shaped it wants to speak to us as well.

But we have nearly lost the way to this holy ground. Too often, we have poisoned or strangled it, or paved over the tracks of the ancient ones. We need a pilgrimage to heal the earth. Our daily news tells us why: to clean up the toxicity of our bomb factories will require over 100 billion dollars; radioactivity from the Hanford, Washington, plant once spread out fifteen miles; some reached the Columbia River, one of the world's premier salmon runs, and a source of irrigation for two states. Department of Energy officials now publicly admit that there have been radiation leaks at Hanford. Michael Lawrence, manager at the facility, says:

> A dangerous buildup of hydrogen gas in nuclear waste storage tanks at the Hanford Nuclear Reservation could explode, sending millions of gallons of radioactive material into the air. We do not believe there is an imminent hazard. We have history on our side, but that's not very comforting.

Underground nuclear explosions have contaminated Nevada aquifers; chemicals have made some Great Lakes fish dangerous to eat; hospital wastes pollute the Atlantic shores; hazardous waste sites like Love Canal dot the landscape threatening the health of our children.

Can the spiritual journeys of the first Americans help us appreciate and care for the earth? The Catholic Church says we should respect what others hold sacred and Vatican Council II reminds us that "... other religions to be found everywhere strive variously to answer the restless searchings of the human heart.... The Catholic Church rejects nothing which is true and holy in these religions" (Declaration on Non-Christian Religions).

To seek what is true and holy in our North American heritage, come and walk an ancient path to a sanctuary in a hidden place. Here, long before the settlers traveled North American trails, or their descendants poisoned the earth, the Pueblo Indians stood on holy ground under father sky and revered mother earth.

The pilgrimage to this healing sanctuary winds over a dusty New Mexico road. It passes through a holy gate, and a holy door, and it leads to sacred earth, the site of the Sanctuario de Chimayo. In this remote settlement between Santa Fe and Taos, New Mexico, Native Americans, conquistadors, and modern Americans have all left their footprints. In the adobe church the Native American reverence for the earth connects with our Christian heritage.

It is called "the Lourdes of the southwest" although pilgrims come not for blessed water, but for blessed dirt. At Easter, as many as twenty-five thousand gather here. Some leave crutches as a testimony of a cure.

Pilgrims enter the shrine through a courtyard framed by an adobe arch. The path leads downward into the church passing through the dark portal. On going in you have the feeling of entering into the depths of the earth. A beautiful altar and crucifix rest at the center. There is also a hole scooped out of the dirt floor. For over a century the devout have come here to venerate the cross and scoop up blessed dirt.

However, long before the church was built here, this spot was a healing spa for the Pueblo Indians. Dimmed by antiquity, there is also a link between this holy place and a similar shrine in Central America. In the early days of the Spanish conquest in Guatemala, a statue of Christ was carved out of balsam and orangewood in the village of Santiago de Esquipulas. The natives loved it because its color resembled their skin color. Over the years, this corpus mounted on a green cross became black from the smoke of incense. The crucifix was put in a shrine close to an ancient Indian spring with health giving properties. Because the Archbishop of Guatemala received a cure there, a chapel was built and it became a shrine.

A custom grew up of making small clay tablets called "benitos" or "tierra del Santo" (holy earth). These cakes made from white clay were embossed with images of the Virgin, the saints, or the crucifix of Esquipulas. Some were eaten, or dissolved in water to be drunk for curative effects. Clay eating, strange to the modern mind, perhaps spoke to the innocence of the earth in those earlier days.

The story of Chimayo is related to that of Esquipulas by a thread that runs through oral tradition—a crucifix like that of Esquipulas was found in the earth at Chimayo. Every time it was taken away it returned. Eventually a chapel was built on that spot and the crucifix enshrined.

In the church at Chimayo one senses the sacred. The faces of the pilgrims reflect reverence. One can almost feel the atmosphere of prayer as that earth is carefully scooped up and taken home as a blessing.

Jesus did not discount the blessedness of earth—for him too, earth was meant to be a blessing. John tells us that "he spat on the ground and made clay of the spittle and anointed the man's eyes with the clay" (Jn 9:6).

The adobe church at Chimayo is a place of beauty and peace. Its brown walls are surrounded by a green oasis. As the eye lifts to the horizon, yellow rock cliffs fade into pink and finally purple at the skyline.

A blind pilgrim left a poem before Our Lady's picture which ends this way:

> In the dusty roads of Chimayo little children with
>   brown faces smile
> when the day is done the sun falls asleep without
>   regret.
> Sleeping in the twinkle of a starry, starry night,
>   it's that old country feeling in Chimayo.
> In all the places of the world I've been, this must
>   be heaven.

At this place, earth, sky, trees, and adobe are in harmony. Because it is a sanctuary of peace and healing, a new tradition has begun—an annual prayer pilgrimage for peace. The road from this healthy site leads to Trinity, New Mexico, where the earth was scorched and melted by the first atomic explosion. It also leads to Los Alamos where war in the stars may be crafted.

On a recent pilgrimage runners were sent from Chimayo to Trinity carrying healing soil and a flaming torch. This flame came from a torch that was relayed around the world during the United Nations Year of Peace in 1986. It is now kept burning continuously at five locations around the world, including El Sanctuario de Chimayo.

Seven hundred people made the pilgrimage. Bishop Donald Pelotte, the first Native American Catholic bishop, led the opening prayer. He prayed for a change of heart—that we cease spending more money for weapons than we do for human needs. He told of Native American Vietnam veterans standing in line at a soup kitchen in Gallup. Despite millions of dollars spent on weapons systems in New Mexico, the state remains one of the poorest in the nation.

The words of the prophet are applicable to our day and our place:

> The earth mourns and withers, the world languishes and withers; the heavens languish together with the earth. The earth lies polluted under its inhabitants; for they have transgressed the laws, violated the statutes, broken the everlasting covenant. Therefore a curse devours the earth (Is 24:4–6).

When the pilgrims arrive at Trinity, where the earth lies polluted, there is a healing blessing for the injured earth. Juan Pecos from the Jemez Tribe casts the blessed soil from El Chimayo in four directions. It is the pilgrims' gift to the suffering earth.

Long ago, Chief Seathl prayed to the four directions and begged the newcomers to care for the land "as we have cared for it." Many did. Many forgot. Some remember today.

The white man took the land at a fearful price to the Native Americans. The Sand Creek incident is one in a long litany of woe. There the earth was stained red with the blood of 105 Indian women and children massacred and mutilated by white soldiers as they stood around a flag of truce. No wonder that Native Americans in our day sometimes offer prayers of exorcism over the land their ancestors cherished.

Now the earth itself faces massacre from the new American. Out on the plains, a nuclear waste dump is housed where once the buffalo roamed. Further east in the farm belt, many homesteaders did remember the sacredness of the land and passed on a sense of stewardship from generation to generation. However, in recent decades, agribusinesses and large corporate farms often break down the links between families and the land. They account to their stockholders rather than to succeeding generations. They do not answer to the long-term fertility of the earth. Large scale high-tech farming has produced bumper crops for a hungry world, but the massive use of pesticides and other chemicals has begun to pollute streams, aquifers, and wells. Poison now flows through the circle of life.

These results are beginning to raise concerns. Travelers across America are impressed by the almost idyllic landmarks: the red barns on the rich farms of Pennsylvania, the wheat fields of Alberta, the corn and soybeans of the heartland, and the cotton fields of the south. But there is an uneasy stirring behind the fence rows. Prophets are raising their voices to demand a healthier agriculture. *The Wall Street Journal* reports:

> All over the farm belt, a scattered movement toward cutting costs and chemical use in favor of more natural methods of farming is cultivating discord among farmers. . . . The scattered movement called "sustainable agriculture" advocates less commercial fertilizer and pesticide use, more crop rotation, and greater use of natural materials to control pests and nourish the land.

One such prophet is David Michaelson of Dawson, Minnesota. He farms part of his land the modern chemical way; another part with a minimum of technological help. Dave wants to continue to raise bumper crops for a hungry humanity, but in a way that will not ultimately poison the earth. Some of his neighbors scoff. Others wonder. A local observer comments that "sometimes Dave is just too far ahead for the average human being in western Minnesota."

Wendell Berry is another prophet who speaks out for the land. He is a Kentucky farmer, poet, philosopher, author, and critic of prevailing culture. For Berry, human salvation or extinction is tied to the land. In fact, he believes it is impossible for us to fulfill the basic biblical command of love for God, neighbor, and self unless we nourish and cherish the land. He writes in *The Unsettling of America, Culture and Agriculture*:

> What connections or responsibilities do we maintain between our bodies and the earth? These are religious questions... no matter how urban our life, our bodies live by farming; we come from the earth and return to it, and so we live in agriculture as we live in the flesh.

Berry believes that the survival of earth depends on each of us living "responsibly in some part of it." He believes at present we are all engaged in a process of poisoning the earth and destroying ourselves in the process. The earth's well-being and ours is inseparable.

The prophets of the land seem to be crying out; "We are out of sync with the cycle of life; we have enshrined death." Somewhere along our pilgrimage we have become uprooted from the very source of our life. In the past, when family farms were passed down from generation to generation the biblical theology of stewardship protected it for the next generation.

The land of our ancestors is always holy to people who remember. It gave them the life force to pass on to us. It nourishes our roots. To return to the "holy ground" of our ancestors is a religious experience.

One Irish American describes his return to the "old sod" as such a pilgrimage:

> On a trip to Ireland, I looked for my family roots in County Cavan. I was hopelessly lost on a narrow road, winding through a maze of hedgerows. Suddenly, two small figures emerged over the crown of the hill. They were the first humans I had spotted along this back road. As they passed, I shouted, "Would you know where the Garahans live?"
>
> "Well we should; you yourself is talkin' to their children!" When they took me into their yard, the friendly, lush earth seemed to sing a welcome. The long line of ancestor Celts, stretching back to the druids, have faded into the mists, but their land—my land—was there to welcome me.
>
> Later, Paddy Sheehan took me to their ancient burial ground, a cemetery five hundred years old. Here, I could experience what the Native Americans understood so well: connectedness.
>
> I have a friend from Canada who spent a whole vacation searching the cemeteries of Ontario for his immigrant ancestors. When he found them, he dug up a little sod and mailed it to his brother and sister with the message, "some holy ground from which we came."

We all have our roots in earth. Jesus was rooted in Mary, and Mary was nourished and given life by fertile Galilee. Where land is treasured and cared for, it is a blessing for future ages. When it is abused, it becomes a curse for future generations.

The segments that follow are about summer's healing beauty—about people being healed and healing the earth. They are about cherishing the lowly, about getting down to earth which is a primary spiritual task on the Christian journey.

It is only when one loves life and the earth so much that without them everything seems to be over, that one can believe in the resurrection and a new world.

— Dietrich Bonhoeffer, *Letters and Papers from Prison*

IMAGINE: A favorite outdoor summertime place of refreshment and enjoyment. Place yourself there. Let it soothe you.

JOURNAL: Getting down to earth is a primary spiritual task on the Christian journey. I need to get back to earth by . . .

INTERSTATE 80

We speed down I–80
65 m.p.h.— not fast enough,
our lives a blur
"I wish I could, but I don't have time!"

    Lord, slow us down;
    bring us back to our senses,
    down to earth,
    back to beauty!

Lead us off the fast lane
down the off-ramp,
into the green meadows of healing summer.

Beauty of Holy Land
Medicine Man

There was a rich man, who was clothed in purple and fine linen and who feasted sumptuously every day. And at his gate lay a poor man named Lazarus, full of sores.

— Luke 16:19–20

Near a mighty cleft in the earth the summer thunderheads pile high and lightning flashes into the depths. It is the meeting camp of father sky and mother earth. It is a deep well of enormous energy and fierce beauty. The great naturalist John Muir wrote:

No matter how far you have wandered hitherto, or how many famous gorges and valleys you have seen, this one, the Grand Canyon of the Colorado, will seem as novel to you, as unearthly in the color and grandeur and quantity of its architecture, as if you had found it after death, on some other star (*Atlantic Monthly*, January, 1898).

It is 217 miles long, up to 18 miles across, and a mile deep. The Grand Canyon is nature's great cathedral, and upon its walls are traced the history of mother earth. Frank Waters, writing in *Arizona Highways*, relates that:

The compressed, twisted, and folded layers of its rock walls . . . reveal the great geologic eras and ages of the earth measured in hundreds of millions of years. From the Cenozoic or Modern era on top—with its brief one million (year) age of man—we read down through the periods

143

of reptiles and dinosaurs, fishes, toothed birds, and land plants, to the oldest Archeozoic era. Here protrudes part of the earth's original crust formed before the planet had cooled.

Like a colorful crescent, Native American lands circle from north to south around the Grand Canyon. This is the land of the Hulapiim, Paiutes, Navaho, Hopi, Apache, Pima, and Papago.

On a September evening, 10,000 representatives from these tribes and more gathered in Phoenix for an important council. Pope John Paul II came from the east out of the sky, and the native peoples came from north and south, from the deserts and mountains, and from the great canyon.

As the pope entered the auditorium, he was accompanied by Bishop Donald Pelotte, the first Native American Catholic bishop. No white man walking with a red man ever received a more thunderous welcome.

It was not always so. Throughout history, whites meeting in council with Native Americans have taken the very best from the natives and handed them the worst of white culture. They treated the Native Americans like Lazarus in the gospel. "There was a rich man, who was clothed in purple and fine linen and who feasted sumptuously every day. And at his gate lay a poor man named Lazarus" (Lk 16:19–20). They were placed outside the gates, while the whites plundered and feasted sumptuously within. Unlike Lazarus, these proud native peoples did not come to this council to beg from the white man, but rather to bless and be blessed by a holy man bringing powerful healing medicine.

Young Native Americans danced a circle dance around the Holy Father and then he brought good medicine from the center of the circle:

It is time to think of the present and of the future. Today, people are realizing more and more clearly that we all belong to one human family, and are meant to walk and work together in mutual respect, understanding, trust, and love. Within this family each people preserves and expresses its own identity and enriches others with its gifts of culture, tradition, customs, stories, song, dance, art, and skills.

Then, standing under a diamond pointing to the four cardinal directions, Emmet White, Pima medicine man, and a member of Saint Peter's parish, raised up a sacred eagle feather and blessed the Holy Father. The auditorium was hushed. John Paul, a representative of the transcendent, had come a long way from Poland and from Rome. He had come like an eagle out of the skies. Emmet White, a representative of the immanent, had also come a long way. He journeyed in the footprints and prayer prints of the most ancient pray-ers on the North American continent. The tracks of his ancestors came down from the mountains, through the great canyon, and across the deserts.

A year later, Emmet White was interviewed about his own spiritual journey as a medicine man. It began with his birth on the reservation in 1938. This is his story:

The call to be a medicine man, I experienced early in my life when I began to ask questions of my father and to feel a connection with my ancestors.

When I reached young manhood, I spent eight years in the Marines. Somewhere along the line alcohol turned from a friend into a tyrant in my life.

When I got out of the service, I drove a truck for a living and had lots of time to myself.

During those long hours on the road, many questions would come to me: "Am I supposed to do more with my life?" "What would it be?" "If I am supposed to do more, can I possibly do it and keep on drinking?"

Along with the questions came feelings. I kept feeling a deep need to do something for my people.

When I got off the road and slept I would have big dreams. In my sleep I was taken on journeys. Four elders would huddle and confer, with me looking on from the outside of the circle. Then they would come and tell me that the healing power would eventually come to me, at a time when things would be right. It was eight years later that I received an eagle feather from a friend in Canada. That was the right time. I knew then that I had to step out and help those who would come to me with illnesses. I began to do what I was told to do in a way that I believe our people used to do. But first I had to go through the pain and hurt and negative feelings about my drinking and my past life . . . and even hurtful and negative feelings about God. I also had to learn to forgive myself.

Out of his own brokenness, Emmet emerged as a medicine man for his people, and more and more people who were sick and hurting sought him out. They were responding to him as a healer with good medicine.

Years later, when Pope John Paul II visited Arizona and held council with the Native Americans, Emmet, a Catholic and a medicine man, was chosen to welcome him.

I was selected by my peers from the southwest to be with the pope. The four elders told me in my dreams, "It is time." If you say yes, you must carry the weight of your people upon your back, so I said "yes" to the pope.

When I blessed him, even though I spoke a different language, it was he and I, and he knew what was happening. I was pleased with his openness to Native Americans. This was the culmination of my hurtful journey of the past, and I knew better things would follow. My friend and my eight-year-old son were there with me. The pope kissed my son on the forehead. He now helps me in my healings.

In the olden days, people would call me and I would go off to a party; now they call me and I go off to heal. If I am asked to sing in church, I sing. It is the opposite kind of calling from what I answered in my early life.

I am called to the circle of healing. The circle is important to native peoples. Our homes used to be round. Our dances and our songs go round. People now are too much out of the circle. When we danced in a circle on the land and sang to the earth and to the animals there was a circle community. Now, we no longer sing to the animals and the plants, and the earth is unhappy. The flowers are saying, "What will happen to us?" Go to Los Angeles and stand on a hill overlooking the smog. The flowers are gone. Now people are starting to say, "What will happen to us?"

When we built our hospital, we prayed over the earth, asking permission to dig before we cut into the mother earth.

We got permission. We need to do that for everything. We need to get down to earth. We do not own it and need to walk with and pray with it.

We are given choices in our lives. In our youth, our road is like a freeway; we can veer and change lanes, but after awhile it narrows into three ways and into two ways, and if we keep saying yes, into a narrow path, and it's difficult to stay on that road. Several times in our life, we have to decide on the road. It is the same even for the pope. If he says yes to being pope then he will have to follow that road. For him and for us our road becomes a little path that we follow. My path has narrowed down into the trail of a medicine man. I am with my people in their pain and with our mother the earth in hers.

Such is the story of the medicine man who blessed the pope. It all happened on a day when the Vicar of Christ came from the skies and the medicine man from mother earth and they exchanged blessings.

IMAGINE: Your ever-narrowing road on mother earth. Follow it. What do you discover along the way?

JOURNAL: On my road, I want to say yes to . . .

Beauty of Holy Land
Healing Artwork

Jesus bent down, and wrote with his finger on
the ground.

— John 8:8

Summer is a time of coloring—green fields, grey edged
thunderclouds, red splashed sunsets, leaping blue waters, golden fields of grain. Summer's scenes are to be
savored and then stored away in the mind's closets for
winter unfolding.

The artist encounters summer beauty. They play
together. Beauty eases in through the doorways of the
senses and skips down the stairwell of the unconscious.
Beauty dances with the inner child, only to emerge another time in brand new garb. Through the artist's
hands, creative beauty is spun again. In this spinning,
there is a new creation, and a power for healing.

When our senses fail to really see, to feel, and to
touch, and when we give up playing with creating, our
world can become the blurred countryside we see at 65
m.p.h. from the highway. Sometimes, on our fast track,
our relationships blur. Jeannie's story is about becoming "unblurred," about sensing, about creating, about
healing.

A divine child lives within us that must be
birthed, that must be heard in order to be whole.
My own journey of healing means coming to
know this divine offspring, listening to the inner voice, and watching the paintings that come.

It does not happen by trying harder; it can only be born by letting go.

Last summer, I celebrated my healing journey at the pilgrimage shrine of Chimayo. I had been there years before, but the doors had been locked. I was not ready to go in then anyway. But last spring, I was. I entered the healing room with the hole in the dirt floor. My friend and I put some dirt on each other; it felt good on my tense neck. I felt blessed by that ritual and by the native art in the chapel. I did not know at that time that I would eventually be a Catholic. I said to God: "Whatever!" It was my prayer of letting go.

You know, you enter the church there by walking down into the earth. When we came out of the chapel into the sun, there was a spirited white horse running free on the hillside nearby. Images of Chimayo have remained with me—the brown earth in the chapel, the green hillside, the white horse. They keep reminding me that life is wonderful; the earth wants to give us delight.

For too long I had forgotten this. I knew no peace. I knew no comfort. I knew no relief. For twenty-three years of my life, I knew frightening, violent headaches, and immobilizing fatigue. As a single parent, I asked God's help in parenting my children and got it; I asked for guidance in my business, and got it. I begged for delivery from the pain but got no answer. No was the answer.

I went to church, retreats, seminars, lectures. I read books, I listened to tapes. I grew, but my heart hurt as well as my head. Batteries of physicians, specialists, counselors could not heal me, so medication was a necessity. Without the prescription drugs, the pain was beyond my endurance. At age forty-seven I was horrified to come face to face with my addiction.

A friend suggested a drug abuse treatment center. I called and told them I needed a way out of the terrorizing pain so I wouldn't need medication. Though physical pain was not their usual focus, they were willing to work with me. At the center, I was asked to make a stick-figure drawing of my family. My dad sat in his leather chair, off to himself behind a newspaper. My grandmother sat fixed at her sewing machine with a paralyzed neck and headache. My sisters and I sat on the floor nearby, sewing things, while mother roared around us with the vacuum.

There it was on paper, my first encounter with myself and family through a drawing. Five mute females, who believed that their entire security rested in "not upsetting daddy." This wasn't new information; the surprise was in the impact. I could see the distancing, the diverting of emotions.

A couple of weeks later, we were asked to visualize and draw our shame, the thing that kept us from loving ourselves and trusting God. My heart felt ponderous as I considered what that looked like—a soft and heavy heart shape, vibrating with dark colors, with smaller lead-weight hearts, like tentacles on a jelly fish. This was my first expression of pain through a drawing. Loving, caring people began to teach me the magic of self-acceptance. It was hard to see what this had to do with headaches and fatigue, but I knew a morbid grasping for approval and security had caused me to be dishonest. I denied I had needs, preferring to take care of a man and his needs so he would take care of me. And then

I was angry inside because men didn't sacrifice themselves for me like I did for them. At age twenty-six, my head had begun to pound and pound. Faulty thinking nearly killed me. In treatment, I gave up the "nicey-nice" game as best I could, daring to peer into the darkness called reality. I began to get well when I began to get real.

I had been an interior designer, but allergies to the petrochemicals in materials forced me out of that field. After my divorce, I returned to school. As a requirement to enter a degree program, I was asked to create a nonverbal autobiography. I decided to use paint chips arranged along a life line. The placement as well as the colors would indicate highs and lows. I had fun gathering the colors and pasting them down. Yet, it was more. I found myself dissolved in tears and touching painful realities that had not yet come up in words. Joy, pain, and grief surfaced in varying intensities as I placed the colors.

I was again being cleansed and renewed through an art project. I experienced a new level of healing by putting my hands to the task. Clearly, there were whole other worlds in which the soul could express itself and be healed.

The next semester I took an art therapy course. The instructor let us know that no one would be reading our minds. Our work was ours. She also let us know that the process of creating was as important as the product. This was a new idea to me; before I had always been product oriented. She honored our creative spirit. We could use anything we liked—poster paint, pastels, clay, charcoal, finger paints.

What did it do for me? I just played like a child, absorbed in creating. I laid aside my design

training to become a little child and found surprising answers. Often my mind was not aware,
but my hands could tell. A sense of the power
grew rapidly within me.

Painting with my nondominant hand encouraged me to let go of control. For me, these
were experiences of meditation and prayer. It
was prayerful sign language between me and the
spirit within.

There have been other essential steps on my
healing journey. The twelve-step recovery approach of AA taught me that we have a divine
power within enabling us to be free. It put God
at the center. We addicts are a sensitive lot whose
bodies do not have a healthy production of natural pain retardants. We are wounded and in need
of God's help.

Our hearts hurt as we long to feel acceptable and loved. Left to our own devices, we tend
to gravitate toward painful relationships rather
than those of joy. Instead of holding still, we rush
around. We too often shut off the inner voice.

The spirit within is creative. I'm glad I listened with my hands.

IMAGINE: Jesus drawing on the ground, the adulter-
ous woman thrown in shame before him. What picture
did he draw for her?

JOURNAL: To release the creative child within me, I
might try to . . .

Beauty of Holy Land
The Healing Earth

And they crucified him and divided his garments among them, casting lots for them, to decide what each should take.

— Mark 15:24

Nevada is a state of risks. The lights of the casinos never go out. "Keno mamas" sit like fairy godmothers waving their keno wands, searching for the right numbers. At the slots, the right numbers are the biblical sevens. God created the earth in seven days. Three sevens creates a jackpot at the slots. Aerobic arms crank and crank and sometimes scoop as all heads turn at the sound of jackpot bells.

It's all here: craps, blackjack, poker, and the odds on almost any game being played in North America. It's all about beating the odds and upping the ante.

What carnival is to Rio and South America, Las Vegas is to North America. It helps a lot of folks to forget for a while, and gives them a chance to try and beat the odds. Some do. Most don't. That's what it all comes down to. Take away the glitter, the comedians, the showgirls, and they would still come, each with a hope of beating the odds.

There is another risk in Nevada—for even higher stakes than those in the fabled casinos. Sixty miles straight north, at a turnoff from highway 95 called Mercury, lies an underground labyrinth. Here for years the U.S. government has been upping the ante with underground nuclear testing.

One Sunday I would participate in a vigil at the gate of the test site. Seventy demonstrators would be arrested for illegal trespassing. I remember it vividly.

Coming up highway 95 from Vegas, you know you are getting close to the site when you drive past a government landing strip and control tower. The strip is empty, except for one gigantic black helicopter. It broods on the desert like some prehistoric bird.

On this Sunday, two hundred people gathered at the site to take part in the Nevada Desert Experience, an ongoing "novena" of prayer, procession, and, for some, crossing the "No Trespass" line.

At 9:30, the participants begin to gather in the desert. There is a makeshift camp set up by some who have camped out. They are mostly middle-aged folks. A grey-bearded Mennonite leads some singing. A Franciscan friar arrives with a van load of older folks. Three tour buses pull in and pour out 120 people in their early twenties to mid-thirties. They are all medical students who have left their national convention in Las Vegas to come here and make a statement demanded, they feel, by their medical oath. They gather around a makeshift pole left by previous demonstrators. It is filled with directional markers. One points northeast and says, Houlton, Maine—3250 miles; Rocky River, Ohio—2370 miles. These students are from all over the U.S. and beyond—from the Netherlands, Honduras, Canada, and Nigeria.

A procession is organized and it begins to wind toward the site. It passes through a dark tunnel under the highway and out into the light again. The site is now in clear view, and close at hand. A wire fence stretches across the desert.

A road winds beyond a checkpoint toward the distant horizon. The desert floor gradually climbs and fades into a mountain range that fills the skyline. Where the Shoshone once roamed freely, the U.S. government has restricted 1350 miles of land for underground nuclear testing. Before approaching the checkpoint, a young doctor speaks to the group:

People must know that in the event of World War III and a nuclear exchange between Russia and the United States, the medical profession would be mostly wiped out, and there would be very little we could do for what survivors there would be. There would be eighty severely injured survivors for each available bed. We can prepare for nuclear war. We cannot prepare to heal its wounds. As doctors, we must make people aware of these facts.

A representative of the medical students then reads from the scriptures:

Therefore, behold, I will allure her and bring her into the wilderness, and speak tenderly to her. . . . And I will make for you a covenant on that day with the beasts of the field, the birds of the air, and the creeping things of the ground; and I will abolish the bow, the sword, and war from the land; and I will make you lie down in saftey (Hos 2:14, 18).

Then the med students prayerfully read their statement of purpose at the test site:

As members of humanity, we recognize and affirm our covenantal obligations to provide stewardship over our natural environment. Although from many faith traditions, we are united in common love for the earth, its people, and all of its species. As members of the medical profession, we recognize and affirm our covenantal obligations to prevent disease and to promote the health of the communities and persons we serve. We gather this morning to reject our complicit violation of these covenants. Our presence today renews our commitment to transform that which threatens the health of all that we love, respect, and cherish.

The participants form a large "medicine wheel" circle; they sing, "We are gentle loving people. We are singing for our lives!" On this Palm Sunday around the world Christians are processing into churches with palm branches. The participants in the Nevada Desert Experience receive their palm branches and the procession moves toward the gate of the test site. Uniformed sheriff's deputies block the road. They are mannerly; so are the participants. They advise anyone considering crossing the line that they are trespassers and they will be arrested. Those that prepare to cross advise that they must protest the enormous and continuous "upping the ante" at the test site.

This is no student lark. Seventy-three medical students walk into the test site. The deputies have white plastic hand cuffs. The students stretch out their hands and are bound.

There is an official military observer. He smiles. He holds a clip board and wears black leather gloves, although the desert wind is warm. The students file past a female deputy wearing reflective sun glasses that hide her eyes. One student who does not cross, watches her classmates and begins to cry softly. The trespassers are placed in a stockade and processed. They will receive a citation listing them as "suspects." While this is going on, four other young people on a lark come down the road carrying a home video camera. They pause at a "No Trespassing" sign. Three pose in front of it and one laughingly proclaims: "We're here to ban the bomb. Alleluia and all that stuff!" At the checkpoint they seem surprised to see students there who look just like themselves. They become subdued. After awhile they leave in silence.

I talk to some of the med students when they are released from the stockade. Betsy is a thirty-four-year-old from the University of North Carolina. She holds a beachball globe. Why did she cross the line? "It's pointless to be a physician if you don't care about our world. You can't take an oath to be a physician and then not really care what happens to the earth."

Shelby is twenty-four and a student at U.C.L.A. "I tried to get involved in my L.A. parish, but found no kindred spirits. I was surprised to find some priests here, two Franciscans even crossing the line. I didn't know priests cared about these sorts of things. Am I concerned about my arrest and its effect on my future career? No, I think it has galvanized me; it's heightened my sense of social responsibility."

At the very hour that Shelby spoke, a high ranking churchman gave a nuanced appraisal at Georgetown University of the policy of mutually assured destruction which makes it necessary to check out bigger and better explosions in Nevada. He said he did not think it was possible to absolutely rule out such deterrents which would be based on a balance of terror even while genuine steps were being taken toward disarmament. On this issue, as on many other complicated issues, intelligent people of goodwill come up with differing practical appraisals on what is the best moral decision. This theologian had come a long way from Europe to present his nuanced view. Betsy and Shelby had also come a long way to Nevada to put their own views on the line.

They were convinced that deadly contamination was being blasted into the Nevada underground, threatening adjoining aquifers with radiation. They believed that relentlessly preparing ever greater nuclear firepower was an issue that violated the very essence of the healing profession.

Back in Las Vegas those taking risks in the casinos could rest easy. The tests aren't conducted when the wind blows their direction.

IMAGINE: The scene at Mercury, the tied wrists of the med students; then imagine Christ before the Roman Tribune, his wrists bound. Hear the question that echoes down the ages: "What is truth?"

JOURNAL: To seek the truth I must sometimes risk . . .

Beauty of Holy Land

Redwoods and the Little Ones

Truly, truly, I say to you, unless a grain of wheat falls into the earth and dies, it remains alone; but if it dies, it bears much fruit.

— John 12:24

One of the greatest summer tourist attractions in North America are the redwood trees on the coast of northern California and Oregon. A thin coastal strip of land, no wider than thirty miles, is the remaining habitat for the remnant of the world's tallest trees.

The life of these redwoods is both ancient and precarious. Its minuscule seedlings find life hard to come by. Bacteria and fungi on the thick forest floor hinder their taking root. But the seeds struggle and adapt. They sprout, and from such tiny seeds—125,000 weigh only a pound—grow giants such as the tallest one, a record 367.8 feet, near Eureka, California.

One day, a tiny seed came skydiving into a nature observer's hand while he was walking through a stand of redwoods. As he dropped it to the ground, he remarked, "All of the potential that is in that tiny seed! Chances are it will not take root. Its existence is so minuscule compared to these centuries-old giants. And yet this seed is sequoia semper virens—it's a redwood seed. What great dignity just to be that! There is a hint of eternity built into its genetic code."

The redwood and its seed offer us a metaphor for human potential. What great dignity to be human, no matter how small or insignificant; no matter how towering or accomplished be other humans.

Anowim

In the New Testament, the little ones of small account are called the "anowim." It is not so far from these redwood trees that the drama of modern anowim—little seeds—is played out. John and Laura can tell you of the little ones. They are foster parents to an AIDS baby. Many of the children of drug addicts are born with AIDS related symptoms. About half grow out of the symptoms; the other become terminal AIDS patients. If the child becomes HIV negative, it is usually moved to a permanent home; if the child is terminal, the foster parents see the little one die a slow death. In a culture that values production and accomplishment, the accomplishment of the AIDS victim is in the hint of the eternal, in the gift left with the caregiver. The soil of foster love that accepts them is very good soil indeed.

Father John lives very close to Muir Woods on one of the hills of San Francisco, at KAIROS House. KAIROS means the center point. One day an interviewer went to visit him and parked his car on a seemingly perpendicular hill. As he got out, the steering wheel locked and wouldn't turn in any direction. A few minutes after meeting Father John, he expressed his anxiety about the locked wheel. Father John put the problem in perspective, "Hey . . . last night I stood by the bed of a twenty-three-year-old fellow whose life slipped away right before my eyes. Don't worry about that locked wheel."

Father John went on to say that AIDS has been a teacher.

It teaches the brevity of life. So many young have died. We take life for granted. We've swept death under the rug in our society.

I visit a hospice every night where most of the patients are young men dying of AIDS. They are the anowim. I try to give them unconditional love. Many have never known it. They have been categorized and labeled. But I find when I send out compassion to them, it comes back.

A while ago, we had a young man in the hospice who was excessively angry. But we just kept accepting him where he was. Twenty-four hours before he died, he reconciled with his sister. He stopped lashing out.

There's a great beauty in the AIDS caregivers too. We take all caregivers for granted don't we?—from the guy who cleans our streets to the nurse who binds our wounds. That's why we have KAIROS House, to provide support to caregivers. The role of caregiver is extremely stressful, calling for intense motivation, heroic dedication, sensitivity, and courage. Without a center of strength within and a sense of humor, it is an impossible task after a time.

I believe the church is powerful when it is with the little ones instead of busy labeling them. We'll all be little ones someday, won't we? We all have to enter the poverty of death. The anowim offer a great gift to the church. They call the church to be a servant . . . not judge. They call forth the footwashing Christ. That's what Christ told us to do, to wash feet.

They also teach us who travel on the high-powered fast lanes of success, money, and comfort that time is slipping away.

Father John walked down the steps of the old Victorian house called KAIROS with the interviewer. It was a glorious summer day. One could look down the hill all the way to the sparkling bay.

"Hey, I'd better come with you and see if I can help you loosen that locked steering wheel of yours!" John got in and jiggled the steering wheel a bit and it unlocked. "Well, that wasn't such a big problem was it?"

As he drove away, summer seemed lovelier, the air fresher, the streets cleaner, the trees more beautiful than when he came. But perhaps the interviewer just hadn't noticed.

Peter calls himself a "nobody—just a podunk guy," but he has spearheaded a group of seven "ordinary citizens" who have determined to send life, not death, to Central and South America.

We adopted a Guatemalan child. It was the beginning of the poor teaching us. Did you know that there are one hundred million abandoned children from the Rio Grande to the tip of South America? How come? Many reasons. A population explosion. Dirt grinding poverty. The oppression of women. The macho, male dominated economic and social systems that won't make room for these kids. Many women are abandoned; but if a new man moves in with such a woman he will not accept the children. So the children are scattered everywhere. The possibilities for helping the little ones down there are limitless. Our little group has helped Fr. Pat Henry open an orphanage in La Paz. It started with ten adolescent boys in the top floor of a building. On the main floor, they're taught woodworking; in three years, they can be self-supporting. The majority of the people in most of these countries are kids. Can we write them off and call ourselves Christian?

IMAGINE: The redwood seed, falling to the ground, resting there, looking for hospitable soil. What else does this image bring to mind?

JOURNAL: I am closest to the foot-washing Christ when I. . .

SEQUOIA SEMPER VIRENS

Redwoods ever verdant,
    always climbing.
Scorched by ancient summer fire,
    stretching up beyond those
    nips at your heels.
Filigreed with dappled sun,
    ferns and mosses feast in your
    eternal shade.

Cut down, yet sending up new sprouts,
    your severed trunk proclaims:
"I have risen!"

Your will to live finds its own way
    unique cloned conifer,
    up forever!

The Easter story is in stone,
    and book—and in redwoods
    semper virens.

Salisbury, Westminster, Chartres,
    your stone arches do not breathe
    like redwood spires.

REFLECTION QUESTIONS:

1) What are some of your best memories of the good old summertime? When is the summertime in your life? What are its special blessings?

2) When and where was the last time you touched or turned the earth? What feelings did it stir?

3) What trail did your ancestors follow? Reflect on what it must have been like for them.

4) Where is holy ground for you? If you could make a pilgrimage where would you go? Chimayo? The Grand Canyon? The Nevada Test Site? Someplace else? Why?

6

AUTUMN'S VISION QUEST

Where there is no vision, the people get out of hand.

—Proverbs 29:18(JB)

Go back in memory before the white men came to North America. The fiery red sky pulls down the black curtain of night; a bronze-skinned youth perches alone on a mountain top. He huddles in a hole dug into the earth. He is humbled by fasting and prayer and time in the sweat lodge. Above him, the Milky Way is splashed like a cascade of glittering diamonds. He is linked to the cosmos. The rocks, the trees, the eagle, the sky speak to him, show him a path, give him a sacred name and an adult destiny.

This is the vision quest of a young Sioux. It is his passage through the eye of the needle. Everything and everyone is left behind. Purified in the tribe's sweat lodge, he has travelled light. He ascended the mountain a boy; he will descend a man.

From this sacred mountain, the young brave peers down into the abyss of canyons and still deeper into the cave of his unconscious—the shadowy world of dreams and visions. Here, the universe is his teacher. Here, he is in touch with the primal energy of fire, wind, and water. His alphabet, his book, his altar is creation. The cosmos speaks a powerful word as he looks up, down, and around.

Long before the white man came to North America and "discovered" its mountain majesties, these lofty crags and eagle lofts were sacred shrines to the first Americans. Long before the whites surveyed, mapped, mined, and denuded these mountains, the Native Americans were one with them. They felt their power. They loved them and were rewarded with a lover's secrets.

The newcomers now live in cities that spread out from the mountains to the plains, bathed in a choking smog that veils the mountains and the sun.

Most new Americans seldom see the stars. When the sun drops below rims of the concrete canyons, it is hazed out by the exhaust of evening commuters. They jet through multiple time zones, dropping down through brown quilted smog that smothers our cities.

Deep in their hearts, they want life to be better for their children and grandchildren. Yet, also, deep in their hearts, there is a stirring awakening that they are bequeathing polluted waters and a toxic earth.

In the midst of this rushing and consuming, thousands of North Americans have packed their flight bags, jetted across the ocean, and boarded buses to travel to a remote area of Yugoslavia. There, in a remote village next to a holy mountain, they seek a vision.

These pilgrims to a place called Medjugorje have experienced the power of prayer, simplicity, and hospitality from people there who are close to the earth and to God. That in itself is a reward for this contemporary vision quest.

The young Sioux long ago on his mountain top would also have had a memory of a holy woman who some five centuries ago brought a vision of wholeness to her people. She was Buffalo Calf Maiden, and her message was in part:

> The round red stone that I placed at my feet and which I touch now with the pipe symbolizes the earth, your mother and grandmother. It is your living place and a sign to you also that Wakan Tanka has given you a red day and a red road of goodness that you must follow with a pure and humble heart.... You must work daily with prayers and thoughts to purify your spirit and dedicate yourself in service to your family, your people, all mankind, and to the Lord of Being.
>
> — Vinson Brown, *Voices of Earth and Sky*

Out on the rim country of Arizona, there lives another native people who search the skies for visions. The Hopis live on three stone mesas jutting out and overlooking the arid plain. They believe that humans have emerged from an underworld. Since that emergence, they have lived on the heights under the bright sun.

Most Hopis start their day by making an offering of cornmeal to the sun. From their heights they can see the great thunderclouds form and race across the sky. There is much more than meets the eye when they look out at the multiformed clouds and down upon the corn in their fields. A Hopi writing about his land and people, says:

> I dream of it. This place where towering storm clouds reveal unto me their omnipotent powers; where thunder roars out from endless distances;

where lightning shares but a moment of its existence with mine.

— Ramson Lomatewama, *My Land—Hopi*

The Hopis and other Native Americans have been touched by the sun-splashed earth and cloud-shadowed vistas that lead to mystery and prayer. Perhaps we new Americans fit the Hopi legend of humans living underground. *Harper's Index* recently reported that many Americans spend 98 percent of their lives inside of their homes, workplaces, or vehicles. We are imprisoned in our bunkers. We are becoming divorced from the earth and creation.

Once upon a time, the Sioux went to their holy mountain on vision quests; the Hopis still look out from their stone mesas. But for most people today, the luminous dots of television provide their only vision. Television, at its worst, takes us to the pinnacle of the temple and asks that we bow down to worship consumerism, or promises us no pain if we take the right pill or down the best beer. Too often, its vision is not from the mountain top, but from the desert as it panders to the idols that Jesus rejected on his vision quest—pride, power, and greed.

Despite its mind-numbing mediocrity, gold can be panned from its sand. Interspersed between the violence and the greed, we discover comedy and laughter, and sometimes gripping drama.

Can television put us in touch with our deepest myths and wildest dreams? The scenes of humans on the moon lifted our spirits, and the explosion of Challenger alerted us to chaos in the cosmos. When the television camera peers down at earth from space ships, it gives us a new vision of earth. We see our common home in space, our legacy to future generations. It is a precious jewel set against the black depths of space.

Perhaps discriminating use of this medium may be the way in our time to fulfill the biblical injunction to fast.

People are searching for a vision. Some searchers are as close as your parish church. They have come to the community seeking a new vision in unity. They are investigating the Catholic church through the Rite of Christian Initiation of Adults.

Each fall, one pastor tells his people: "You and I are under investigation by the RCIA. These folks are investigating the church, and that's us!" At the end of fall and the beginning of Advent, these newcomers go up to the altar and are enrolled as catechumens. Their coming up is a tentative "yes" to participate in our vision. They are indicating they want to continue to walk with us on a vision quest of faith.

IMAGINE: The primary locale for your own "vision quest." Might it be the TV screen? the morning paper? magazines? books? the movie screen? friends? co-workers? . . . the Bible? What images shape your dreams? your desires?

JOURNAL: When I imagine the images that call me to my truest self, I think of . . .

PRAYER

Christ above me
Christ below me
Christ beyond me
Christ within me.

Arrow to the east - Light!
Arrow to the west - Insight!
Arrow to the north - Wisdom!
Arrow to the south - Humility!

Alpha pushing
Omega pulling
Spirit breathing
Arrow piercing
Lord dancing
Jesus healing.

First Step, Twelfth Step

Come Lord Jesus - Maranatha!

Beauty of the Winds of Change

Desert Breeze

And behold the Lord passed by, and a great and strong wind rent the mountains, and broke in pieces the rocks before the Lord, but the Lord was not in the wind;. . .and after the fire a still small voice.

— I Kgs 19:11, 12

Douglas Boyd writes in *Rolling Thunder* of the wisdom of his people in seeking their roles in life.

We are born with a purpose in life and we have to fulfill that purpose. Some of our young men go out when they are twelve or thirteen years old and pray and fast at a certain sacred place. They learn their purpose in life. Now we hear of the new young people talking about finding their identity, their place in life and they are very wise to do that. . .and they are trying to make things better for other people in life, which is our only purpose in life—to share with others.

The old man sat beneath a palm tree, its fronds rustling in the desert breeze. This was the first week in his life he had not worked. His office at the retreat center was now closed; a recent mild stroke had restricted his work, but not his memory. It ranged over seventy-five years, recalling his childhood in Germany, his immigration to the U.S., and the forty years he had spent as a Franciscan pastor with the Papago Indians in southwest Arizona. Now, in the autumn of his life, he could look back and see more than he saw as he was living it. He now could feel the winds of change that had swept through his life journey—and how critically important it was to understand his purpose in life, even if it was in a direction he hadn't anticipated.

In August of 1939, he had set out from Germany. His destination was Japan where he hoped to spend the rest of his life as a missionary. He was to finish his theology studies in the U.S. on his way, but World War II intervened. In 1941, he found himself marooned in California, a German national, fenced in by the war in Europe and the emerging conflict in the Pacific. So he took a detour. He volunteered for pastoral work in Arizona.

He was assigned to Cowlic, a village of 132 people. From this village, he would ride by horseback as far as fifty miles to visit outlying settlements.

When he first arrived, he spoke very little English, and none of the language of the Papago Indians. He would learn Papago before he would learn English.

Some nuns ran a two-room school so Father Lambert Fremdling, OFM, decided to be taught Papago by the children. Sometimes, the elders would smile as he would repeat a few "naughty words" the children had stirred into his alphabet soup. Since there was no written Papago, he composed his own grammar and dictionary.

He looks back fondly at those early years.

> They taught me before I ever taught them, and that was good. As a stranger, I needed to change more than they. I did, and I saw things differently.
> They were very gentle in their teaching; they would never correct me. I had to trust them and I did. They had a deep reverential attitude toward

the democratic process and they gave me lessons in democracy not to be learned from books. They always sought consensus and never tried to beat down a dissenter. I remember one time they were electing a chief and one man held back his vote. So they selected an interim chief and would come together every year to elect a permanent chief. But the one man would hold out. In the seventh year, the dissenter went out to the desert to gather wood and his wagon tipped over on him and broke his leg. In the hospital, he had time to think and he admitted it was only his stubbornness that had caused him to withhold his vote all those years. He really had nothing against the nominee. He was just being contrary. The others must have realized this, yet they always honored his dissent.

This mutual respect for the dignity and rights of each individual carried over into all meetings and gatherings. Meetings took a long time because each person had the right to speak and be heard. Each did speak and each was heard out with the greatest patience.

Now, looking back, I see that I had lots of preconceived ideas. I had expectations about the behavior of other people. In a sense, I grew up with the Papagos. They taught me simplicity and honesty in dealing with the seeming contradictions and paradoxes of life. To be mature is to live with paradox. And they helped me to mature.

They never got angry with the foibles of their neighbors. They knew how to live with contradictions. Life always seemed to balance out for them.

Some outsiders consider their lifestyle lackadaisical. This was not true at all. They knew how to adapt to the seasons and the weather. They did not give up on projects. They were just patient in accomplishing them in due time.

They have a down-to-earth wisdom and a deeply rooted Catholic faith. The native peoples after all are among the oldest Catholics in North America. The Papagos trace their faith back to Father Kino and the Jesuit missionaries of the seventeenth century.

Too often, their faith sensitivities have not been respected. One example illustrates many others. I once observed a new pastor who came to a Papago parish and was not pleased with a side altar containing many images of their favorite saints. He proceeded to gather up all the images and deposited them in the town dump.

The people later held a procession to the dump, recovered the images and built another chapel for them in another village. Yet, they did not confront the arrogant pastor. It was not an either/or thing with them; it was both/and, living with such a pastor and keeping their images in another place.

With the Papagos, I came to learn the beauty of all things. Everything in nature is really beautiful if we have no preconditions. Preconditions ruin our openness to beauty. That's what the native people have—an openness to beauty. In my early years, I thought a pinto horse and a German Shepherd dog were beautiful. I came to learn that if I am open to see, all horses and dogs are beautiful, each in their own way. The hills of California are just as beautiful in autumn when they are golden as they are in spring when they are green. The native peoples taught me to look at things as they are, not as I expect, or demand them to be.

The breeze stirred the overhead palm. Retreatants walked by and recognized the old priest. He was now the "senex," the mentor, the senior statesman at this renewal center in fashionable Scottsdale. Through his presence, some of the wisdom of the Papagos was being shared.

The winds of change had shifted the direction of his life. He never reached Japan. His vision quest took an unexpected turn. His life journey was through the desert with the Papagos. What did he see now, as he looked back with autumn vision? "The grace of God...conversion; change can come in the circumstances where you are. The circumstances for me were not what I had expected, but grace was where I was—with the Papagos." When he died several months later, Father Lambert whispered his prayers in Papago.

As Father Lambert talked, the desert wind blew through the palms. That same wind just a few miles away shook the wind chimes of Paulo Soleri into tingling song.

In some ways, Paulo was like Lambert, an immigrant who came to the desert from his home in Italy and learned from the land and its people.

Paulo exemplified a vision that "always contains a song." Since 1970, Soleri's cast bronze wind-chimes have helped to finance construction of a dream, an ecologically sound desert city called Arcosanti.

This architectural visionary long ago foresaw that modern urban sprawl and its pollution must evolve into a more livable habitat. His prototype city is evolutionary, the dream of an architect with a mystic's vision. He calls this vision arcology. The *New York Times* reports that "Arcology is a methodology that recognizes the necessity for radical reorganization of the sprawling urban landscape into dense integrated three dimensional towns and cities."

Soleri's model city has begun to rise on the desert near Cordes Junction. It will allow no automobiles, will harness solar power, and will use only 2 percent of the land that is gobbled up by a conventional suburban community of equal population. Early in its development, *Newsweek* called it the most important experiment in urban architecture undertaken in our time.

In some ways, Soleri's Arcosanti is like the saguaro cactus that thrives in the desert. It is upright, efficiently utilizing space and natural resources. It is a preserving creature, adapting to, and conserving the natural landscape.

Soleri's vision quest, like his city, evolved. When he was interviewed some years ago about its slow progress in being built, he indicated things would have to get a lot worse before there would be a turn around in urban planning.

In his later years, Soleri's thinking attempted to bridge ecological-architectural concerns and theology— the city of God and the human city converging.

In 1963 the American Institute of Architects awarded him its Gold Medal of Craftsmanship for his renowned wind bells.

Out on the desert at Arcosanti, Soleri's wind chimes still whisper their song. And where the mission bells toll over the grave of Father Lambert, in the land of the Papago,

> The Papago sternly hold to the belief that visions do not come to the unworthy. But to the . . . humble there comes a dream. And the dream always contains a song.
>
> — Ruth Murray Underhill, *Singing for Power*

IMAGINE: The cactus-studded desert; hear the wind chimes breaking the silence. Do they enliven the desert place in your heart?

JOURNAL: My favorite songs are...
About my quest, they reveal...

Beauty of the Winds
of Change
Committed Visionaries

And it shall come to pass afterward, that I will
pour out my spirit on all flesh; your sons and
your daughters shall prophesy, your old men
shall dream dreams, and your young men shall
see visions. Even upon the menservants and
maidservants in those days, I will pour out my
spirit.

— Joel 2:28–29

Dorothy Day, who died in 1980 at the age of eighty-
three, had a radical vision quest that was rooted in
Matthew 25:40 — "Truly, I say to you, as you did it
to the least of my brethren, you did it to me."

Her vision quest began as a young girl when she
dreamed of becoming a writer who would convince people of the injustice in the world. She died having completed a life that was faithful to her original dream.
She published six books, wrote 1500 articles, and, with
Peter Maurin, left a legacy of fifty Catholic Worker
houses. These houses over the years fed and sheltered
thousands of the anowim and offered friendship and acceptance to "the least of Christ's brothers and sisters."

These statistics however meant little to Dorothy.
She did not reckon with a bookkeeper's mentality. From
the beginning, she marched to a different drummer.

Her early life was without a denominational frame-
work. She found her community in the various radical

movements seeking redress from such social abuses as child labor, worker exploitation, and economic inequity. She was at home with anarchists and socialists. For a while, she was a member of a communist party affiliate group. She was a friend of the hard-drinking playwright Eugene O'Neill and passed through several unhappy love affairs.

She went to Washington, D.C., and was arrested with the suffragettes demonstrating for women's right to vote. She went on a hunger strike and was placed in solitary confinement in the tough Occoquan Prison. In that darkness she turned to the scriptures for a word of hope.

Through a chance meeting with a nun at a beach, she began to read about the Catholic church. Although drawn to the church it presented a dilemma for her: "To become a Catholic would mean for me to give up a mate with whom I was much in love. It got to the point where it was the simple question of whether I chose God or man."

To the dismay of her friends, she made the lonely choice to become a Catholic. It meant climbing a different mountain and incorporating her vision of justice into the Catholic vision. What she saw in the church was muddled. On the one hand, it was a church of the poor immigrant masses but some of its leaders were allied with the rich and the powerful—the very people who kept the poor "in their place."

Dorothy sought a vision of where she might fit into this large and sometimes confusing church. On a pilgrimage—vision quest—to the Shrine of the Immaculate Conception in Washington, D.C., she prayed with great anguish that a door would open that would allow her to use her talents for the poor.

Native Americans on their vision quests were moved by a harbinger, perhaps a majestic eagle, or a wily coyote. Dorothy's messenger turned out to be a dishevelled dreamer named Peter Maurin. Out of their new friendship *The Catholic Worker* newspaper was born. Its philosophy was summed up by Peter when he wrote: "The world would be better off if people tried to become better. And people would be better if they stopped trying to become better off."

Through *The Catholic Worker*, Day and Maurin began a critique of social systems based on gospel ideals. The church had social encyclicals but it needed lay people to apply them to concrete situations. They tried to do that.

Dorothy was also a pacifist. There were two streams of thought in the Catholic tradition regarding war: one was a river that justified most wars; the other was a trickle that opposed all wars. Dorothy stood by the trickle challenging the view that puts security in weapons and identity in power.

Dorothy's bishop, Cardinal Francis Spellman in New York, represented the mainstream, yet he never silenced her; she in turn was loyal to him as her bishop. Throughout her life, she was nourished by daily Mass, recitation of the office, two hours of meditation on the gospels and her daily rosary.

Dorothy's last arrest came at age seventy-five on the picket line with the farm worker activist Cesar Chavez. This woman, who believed that the works of mercy were incompatible with works of war, who lived with the poor and for the poor, was herself an arrow in a circle. Perhaps her vision quest is best summed up in her own words: "The most effective action we can take is to try to conform our lives to the folly of the cross."

In the Book of Genesis, Rachel wept over her own barrenness. In our own time, a modern Rachel wept for the poisoned and potentially barren earth. Her cry may turn out to be the most prophetic of the twentieth century. Rachel Carson was not a likely prophetess. She lived alone and had no position of power, or powerful lobby. Her life was cut short at fifty-seven. Yet through her writing she provided a major vision for our time. Supreme Court Justice William Douglas called her book, *Silent Spring*, "...the most important chronicle of this century for the human race."

Silent Spring challenged the reckless warfare waged upon the environment in the name of progress:

> The most alarming of all man's assaults upon the environment is the contamination of air, earth, rivers, and the sea with dangerous and even lethal materials. . . . In this now universal contamination of the environment, chemicals are the sinister and little recognized partners of radiation in changing the very nature of the world. . . . As Albert Schweitzer has said, "Man can hardly even recognize the devils of his own creation."

Silent Spring elicited a firestorm of protest from the chemical industry and other vested interests. But the wraith-like Carson had managed to raise a single voice of alarm that was being heard. At the end of her testimony before a senate committee, Senator Gruening of Alaska looked across the conference table and said: "Miss Carson, every once in awhile, in the history of mankind, a book has appeared which has substantially altered the course of history. . . . Your book is of that important character."

In the Hebrew Testament Rachel cried for life. Rachel's crying brought fruitfulness. *Silent Spring* was a vision quest for a fruitful earth and deliverance from the jaws of death. To modern men and women "who scarcely recognize the devils" of their own creation, she offered exorcism and a better vision.

You have heard that it was said, "You shall love your neighbor and hate your enemy." But I say to you, love your enemies (Mt 5:43–44).

After the defeat of Japan in 1945, General Douglas MacArthur, the Allied commander-in-chief in the Pacific, was selected to bring military occupation to Japan. The Japanese, stunned and cowed in defeat, could only fear harsh retribution from the enigmatic and imperious MacArthur.

From his childhood at a military post on the frontier to his graduation from West Point and forty-year military career, he had been trained for war. He had been a proud warrior whom the Japanese had humiliated in the Philippines in 1941. Now they fully expected a wrathful warrior's revenge.

Instead of exploitation and humiliation they received reconciliation and friendship. No one in the twentieth century was a more surprising visionary than this army general. From the moment he stepped on Japanese soil, MacArthur had a better vision for a new Japan: a nation less militaristic, more peaceful, a friend among the nations. His vision quest would bring democracy—not terror—to a feudal empire.

Although he insisted that the emperor was not divine, he allowed him to keep his ceremonial role. At the same time he introduced women's rights, labor unions, land reform, and a massive public-health program that saved more lives than had been lost in the war. He backed social security legislation and redistributed 90 percent of the feudal land to the peasants.

On September 2, 1945, the chagrinned representatives of the Japanese empire stood on the decks of the battleship Missouri, waiting to sign the documents of surrender. MacArthur, wearing none of his ribbons and decorations, addressed them:

> It would be inappropriate... to meet in a spirit of distrust, malice, or hatred... instead both conquerors and conquered must rise to that high dignity which alone benefits the sacred purposes we are about to serve.... [It is my] earnest hope that a better world would emerge... one founded upon faith and understanding—a world dedicated to the dignity of man and the fulfillment of his most cherished wish—for freedom, tolerance, and justice.
>
> — William Manchester, *The American Caesar*

Thus began the vision quest of MacArthur for his defeated enemies. He wrote some of the key sections of the new Japanese constitution which established democracy. During the war, MacArthur had been informed of the intent to drop nuclear bombs on civilian targets only after the decision was made in Washington. As military governor of Japan he would state that nuclear weapons challenge the reason and the very purpose of mankind.

Douglas MacArthur brought the winds of change to Japan. Because of his vision Japan took her place in the circle of nations as a partner and a friend. One of the lessons to be learned from MacArthur's story is that sometimes visions come from unlikely sources. Despite his setbacks of failed political hopes and the loss of his command in Korea, history rates him as an exceptional general and an amazing statesman. He proved his statesmanship in Japan by living out the gospel injunction, "Love your enemies."

IMAGINE: The scene on the battleship Missouri with the defeated Japanese surrendering to the Allies. If you could insert your enemies in such a scene, what would you say to them?

JOURNAL: Dorothy, Rachel, and Douglas offer our world hope because...

Beauty of the Winds of Change

A Vision of Justice

> Unless your righteousness exceeds that of the scribes and Pharisees, you will never enter the kingdom of heaven. . . leave your gift there before the altar and go; first be reconciled to your brother, and then come and offer your gift.
>
> — Matthew 5:20, 24

In their pastoral letter *Economic Justice for All*, the U.S. Catholic bishops wrote that "The Body of Christ which worshippers receive in communion is also a reminder of the reconciling power of his death on the cross. It empowers them to work to heal the brokenness of society and human relationships and to grow in a spirit of selfgiving to others."

The bishops are visionaries in the search for human justice. They observe the circle of human solidarity misshapened by greed and individualistic preoccupations. They demand concern for the general welfare and challenge us to concern for more than just personal salvation. It is not enough to just go to church and "leave our gift at the altar." They call for reconciliation beyond the altar through the pursuit of justice in our society. Our "circle" is to expand from the altar outward.

Roger Bergman, a writer for *The Catholic Voice* newspaper in Omaha, Nebraska, observes that we are an excessively individualistic people:

187

Increasingly it seems we stray from the vision of the common good. . . . Whether the issue is abortion or poverty we tend not to recognize any "compelling interest" beyond our own immediate interests of career, family, or business. It's as if we were losing the capacity to imagine a just society.

To imagine a just society demands a vision quest that widens the circle. It requires creativity to imagine what a just society would really look like. The bishops of North, Central, and South America have all pursued such a quest.

As long ago as 1919 the American Bishops Program of Social Reconstruction sought the introduction of a minimum wage, child labor laws, the right to unionize, restrictions on monopolies, vocational training, health and old age insurance. In 1919 these were just dreams. In recent years, the bishops of the western hemisphere have continued to dream of visions that contain reconciliation, solidarity, and justice.

The Canadian bishops endorse and identify with a compassionate minority:

Across Canada, there are some encouraging signs. . . . A variety of Christian groups have been working with the poor and oppressed peoples of their communities, organizing educational events on issues of injustice and pressing leaders of governments and industries to change policies (although a minority). . . this minority is significant because. . . it is challenging the whole church.

— Canadian Bishops Conference,
A Compassionate Minority

These visions of the Canadian and U.S. bishops no doubt received impetus from the dramatic "preferential option for the poor" espoused by the bishops of South America at Medellin in 1968. In the U.S., the bishops have faced the fact that even when there is recovery and increased employment, the wealthy are getting richer, the middle class is shrinking, and the poor are getting poorer. They have noticed that a nation that spends a high proportion of every tax dollar on military spending and munitions is unable to take the homeless off the streets.

In the face of these circumstances, they have tried to dream a better dream. *Economic Justice for All* was an appeal not only to bring our gifts to the altar, but also to go out from the altar and reconcile the brokenness in society:

> To worship and pray to the God of the universe is to acknowledge that the healing love of God extends to all persons and to every part of existence, including work, leisure, money, economic and political power and their use, and to all those practical policies that either lead to justice or impede it. Therefore when Christians come together in prayer, they make a commitment to carry God's love into all these areas of life (*Economic Justice for All*).

If we were to take the measured words of the bishops' pastoral into the world of dreams, how might they be imaged? What symbols might point to their deep meaning? The native peoples let nature speak to them in their vision quests. What could we learn from the birds and the beasts?

Would the geese flying the central flyway from Canada along the Missouri River tell us something about solidarity and the common good as they take turns in breaking the head winds for each other?

Would the beavers who build habitat not only for themselves but for ducks, frogs, herons, and countless species tell us something about the need for jobs and homes for everyone?

Would the bear who leaves no cubs out in the winter cold tell us something about homelessness?

We must dream of a vast human circle. These are the rational animals doing what ducks, beavers, and bears do, but doing much more. In this circle, the fittest care about the weakest. We can dream what that circle would look like: no homeless sleeping on the streets, no children going to bed hungry, no one without work, and no abuse of our environment.

IMAGINE: A human circle making room for the weakest. Who would you suggest be brought into the circle?

JOURNAL: A simpler lifestyle for me means . . .

Beauty of the Winds of Change

Arrows

> And Jesus, full of the Holy Spirit, returned from
> the Jordan and was led by the Spirit for forty
> days in the wilderness.
>
> — Luke 4:1–2

The autumn winds of change strip the leaves from the aspens and bare the mountains. One can see deeper and farther into the forest, but what view is to be found there? Is the view from autumn's hills and mountains one of beauty, or is the final blaze of color some omen of a final cosmic death? Should the Christian look from the mountains to the next millennium with cynicism or with hope?

Some surveyors see arrows pointing to oblivion. The world wars, the holocaust, Hiroshima, the ravages of drugs, the squandering of planetary and human resources, the gulf between rich and poor point toward the self-destruction of the planet.

Ours may be known as the time when humans come to full awareness of the ecological crisis. As Catholic Christians, will we be part of the problem, or of the solution? Some would lay the problem at our door. They would say that the command of Genesis to "have dominion over the earth" gives biblical sanction to do with the earth as we please, and now we are reaping the whirlwind. John Muir often railed against Christianity's belief in one deity and its focus on the human species.

Arnold Toynbee pins the blame for our ecological crisis on monotheism! We are too concerned with God out there and not concerned enough about earth, right here. Paul Ehrlich faults the church for not sanctioning limitations on birth as a means to restore a balance to the planet.

The fact is we should assume no more nor less of the blame than is our due. Vatican Council II did urge responsible parenting. Beyond whatever our failings might be perceived to be, Catholics have a tradition of eco-spirituality—a faith view that loves and cares for creation. That tradition includes the 1500-year-old Benedictine order which developed a stewardship agriculture and passed on the Rule of Saint Benedict which counseled moderation in all things, not exploitation of all things. The great medieval mystics like Francis of Assisi, Hildegard of Bingen, Julian of Norwich, Mechtilde of Magdeburg, and Meister Eckhart were conscious of the divine presence at the heart of all created reality. Julian's writings are full of the proclamation that our joy is to find the presence of God permeating all creation.

Hildegard, a remarkable eleventh-century abbess, proclaimed: "Just as a circle embraces all that is within it, so does the Godhead embrace all."

In our day, Teilhard de Chardin and Thomas Merton lead us to that same deep reverence for God dwelling at the center of all reality. Merton saw the circle of creation in microcosm within the depths of each person. He saw our spiritual journey as moving toward the true center point at the core of our soul:

The only true joy on earth is to escape from the prison of our own false self, and enter by love into union with the Life Who dwells and sings within the essence of every creature and in the core of our own souls.

— *New Seeds of Contemplation*

Perhaps the best symbol for this tradition of eco-spirituality is the Celtic cross—the cross that intersects the circle; an arrow in the circle of the sun, the moon, and the whole chain of being. It tells us God is beyond us, yet within us.

God in all creatures, God at the center, God in the deepest core—the words of the mystics are part of the Christian tradition of reverencing creation. Perhaps the critics have not pondered them. Perhaps Christians have not either.

Scientists observe another cold wind blowing. Some hold that the universe is winding down and we might be using up all of our sources of energy. We simply might run out of everything.

If the universe is winding down, why be concerned about anything? We are helpless and hopeless from a human standpoint. No wonder we rush madly to consume what we can while we can. The possibility of creating something new and beautiful for the common good gets swept aside by cynicism. The British philosopher Bertrand Russell voiced such cynicism in his book *Why I Am Not A Christian*:

> . . . all the inspiration, all the noonday brightness of human genius are destined to extinction in the vast death of the solar system. . . . Only on the firm foundation of unyielding despair can the soul's habitation henceforth be safely built.

In his book, *The Cosmic Blueprint*, Paul Davies uses the image of two arrows: one arrow points toward degeneration and death. The other points toward hope and renewal—toward a theory that the universe is progressing through the steady growth of structure, organization, and complexity to ever more elaborate states of matter and energy.

As Christians we must look to the cross of Jesus as our arrow of hope and renewal. The arrow of Jesus points toward both the heavens and the earth. St. Paul sees the incarnation of Christ affecting the whole universe:

> He is the image of the invisible God, the first-born of all creation; for in him all things were created, in heaven and on earth, visible and invisible, whether thrones or dominions, or principalities or authorities—all things were created through him and for him. He is before all things, and in him all things hold together. . . . He is the beginning, the first-born from the dead, that in everything he might be pre-eminent. For in him all the fullness of God was pleased to dwell, and through him to reconcile to himself all things, whether on earth or in heaven, making peace by the blood of his cross (Col 1:15–20).

If all things hold together in Christ, then the activity of Christ in all of creation is dynamic. It is going on now. His cross is an arrow that ultimately points to an energy greater than death. Perhaps what we lack are energetic imaginations capable of picturing what his love poured out upon the earth might still produce.

Morton Kelsey, an Episcopal priest and author, takes a copy of the New Testament to many of his conferences. During his talk he will say "if you don't think Jesus was about healing on this earth . . . then look what's left of the New Testament after I've removed all the passages referring to healing!" He then holds up a New Testament that is pretty well shredded.

How might Christ's concern with healing relate to the present ecological crisis? He consistently brought the blind and the lame into his healing circle and used water and earth in some of these healings, symbolizing the connection between the person and the environment. A right connection is essential to healing and well-being. To poison the earth is to hand down a death sentence to future generations. Would not Jesus the healer be concerned about both the earth and our children? In too many places today he could not recommend the sick wash in a nearby pool, nor place mud on a blind person's eyes.

Jesus used the earth, the mountains, and the lake to instruct his disciples. He said "Come and see"—see the lilies of the field, the fruitful vines, the fields ripe for the harvest. He loved the fruitfulness of the earth. He was connected to all of creation. His curse was reserved for the barren fig tree. Would he bless such places as Love Canal, Chernoble, Rocky Flats, Hanford, the Mercury nuclear test site, or the devastated rain forests?

The incarnate son of God took earth seriously. He proclaimed an afterlife, but he lived his life in harmony with nature and created things. The Christian belief in an afterlife in no way demands indifference to the earth.

The Jesus arrow is a dynamic energy that has entered into the circle of matter and human history. It is an arrow that points in the direction of hope and new creation.

As Catholic Christians, we can be open and hopeful to surprise. If we follow the cross, the arrow of hope, we can be pregnant with possibilities.

People are gathering in life circles, base communities, and countless healing circles. They are networking.

The wisdom of the native peoples and the wisdom of women, both so long scorned, is being given its rightful place in the circle.

Television, instead of being a wasteland, might help prevent a wasteland. It is bringing us into a global community. Satellites allow us to spy on the enemy but we see that they are humans like us—dancing, singing, loving their children, mourning their dead. From our orbiting satellites we can see ourselves together on this tiny life-filled circle in space and no boundaries appear.

Perhaps we are beginning to see that we are in this God-given journey together—plants, animals, and mother earth. Up on the mountaintops, in the midst of forest stillness, a fresh wind stirs, and after it, a whisper of a voice:

> Go forth, and stand upon the mount before the Lord. . . [Then there was] a still small voice. And when Elijah heard it, he wrapped his face in his mantle (I Kgs 19:11–13).

IMAGINE: You are on a road going up toward the summit of a mountain. After enjoying the vistas and experiencing the quiet, observe two road signs. One arrow points up with the word HOPE. The arrow on the other sign points backward. Follow the HOPE arrow as it directs you to the top of the mountain. There are people there who smile at you and want to encourage you. Meet them and let them encourage you.

JOURNAL: The image of the earth-circle energizes me for. . .
The image of the Christ-arrow moves me toward. . .

REFLECTION QUESTIONS:

1) What was your vision quest, your rite of passage? Reflect on the changes that took place. Have you followed the path you discovered then?

2) Father Lambert learned from the Papago. Think of people you know who are ethnically or culturally different. What can you learn from them?

3) Are you imprisoned in a bunker? Do you want to take time out to be close to something in nature? Do you ever take such time?

4) Dorothy Day, Rachel Carson, and Douglas MacArthur were visionaries. Think about someone you know who has a hopeful vision. How does this speak to you?

5) Wendell Berry challenges each of us to a better vision where the survival of the earth depends on *each* of us living "responsibly in some part of it." Try to come up with some specific actions you can take toward healing the earth.

6) If you could choose one story or one energy place in this book that helps to give you a hopeful vision quest, which would it be? Why?

RESOURCES

Armstrong, Virginia. *I Have Spoken*. Athens, OH: Ohio University Press (Swallow), 1971.

Bly, Robert. "Surprised by Evening." *Selected Poems*. New York: Harper and Row, 1986.

Bowden, Henry W. *American Indians and Christian Missions*. Chicago, IL: University of Chicago Press, 1985.

Boyd, Douglas. *Rolling Thunder*. New York: Dell Publishing Co., Inc., 1976.

Brown, Joseph Epes. *The Sacred Pipe*. New York: Penguin, 1971.

Brown, Vinson. *Voices of Earth and Sky*. Happy Camp, CA: Naturegraph Pubs., Inc., 1976.

Buck Ghost Horse. *Red Nations Sacred Way*. Printed and distributed by The Institute in Culture and Creation Spirituality, Oakland, CA, 1987.

Carson, Rachel. *Silent Spring*. Boston, MA: Houghton, Mifflin Co., 1987.

Canadian Catholic Bishops. *A Compassionate Minority*. "From Words to Action, on Christian Political and Social Responsibility—Labor Day Message, 1976." Document 44, *Do Justice! The Social Teaching of the Canadian Catholic Bishops (1945-1986)*. E.F. Sheridan, S.J., ed. Sherbrooke, Quebec: Editiones Paulinas and Jesuit Centre for Social Faith and Justice, 1987.

Davies, Paul. *The Cosmic Blueprint*. New York: Simon and Schuster, 1988.

Eaton, Evelyn. *The Shaman and the Medicine Wheel*. Wheaton, IL: Theosophical Publishing House, 1982.

Frost, Robert. "Stopping by Woods on a Snowy Evening." *Poetry of Robert Frost*. Ed. by Edward C. Lathem. New York: Holt, Henry, and Co., 1979.

John Paul I (Albino Luciani). *Illustrissimi.* Boston, MA: Little, Brown and Co., 1978.

Leon-Portilla, Miguel. "The Poem of Ayocuan." *Native Meso-american Spirituality.* Mahwah, NJ: Paulist Press, 1980.

Lomatewama, Ramson. *My Land—Hopi.* Incline Village, NE: Native American Publishing Co., Inc., 1989.

Manchester, William. *The American Caesar.* Boston, MA: Little, Brown and Co., 1978.

Merton, Thomas. *New Seeds of Contemplation.* New York: New Directions, 1961.

Neihardt, John. *Black Elk Speaks.* Lincoln, NE: University of Nebraska Press, 1979.

Rilke, Rainer Maria. *Selected Poems.* Translated by C.F. MacIntyre. Berkeley, CA: University of California Press, 1940.

Rohr, Richard. *Our Lady of Guadalupe: Why the Story Fascinates.* Albuquerque, NM: Center for Action and Contemplation.

Russell, Bertrand. *Why I Am Not a Christian.* London: Allen and Unwin, 1957.

Ryan, "Cookie" Danita Begay. "Kinaalda, the Pathway to Navaho Womanhood." *Native People's Journal of the Heard Museum* (Winter, 1988).

Steinmetz, Paul. *Meditations With Native Americans.* Santa Fe, NM: Bear and Co., Inc., 1984.

Underhill, Ruth Murray. *Singing for Power.* Berkeley, CA: University of California Press, 1968.

U.S. Catholic Bishops. *Economic Justice for All.* Washington, DC: U.S. Catholic Conference, 1986.